"Friendships between women can range from a sisterhood that strengthens the soul to a battleground that leaves us scarred and anything in between. Though we value deep friendships, we've been hurt enough to be jaded. Instead, we stay friendly but distant, trying to avoid the drama. Andi Andrew gets it, but she also understands that our distance holds us back from meaningful relationships. And that's where this book comes in. In *Friendship—It's Complicated*, Andi directly addresses the problems and pain we face in our friendships. Then drawing on biblical insights and personal stories, she offers practical, hard-won wisdom and tools to face our wounds, heal, and learn to build friendships with power and purpose. If you're looking to build healthy friendships, get this book and apply it to your life. Because, as Andi says, 'Friendships are worth the fight,' and they will transform your life."

Jo Saxton, leadership coach, speaker, author of *Ready to Rise*

"Andi Andrew is a powerful leader in the church today, and this book is an example of why. She is truly a master of leading with vulnerability. Reading this book is like sitting down for coffee and having your tenderest friendship wounds feel seen. This message will counsel, console, and commission all who read it; of that I have no doubt."

Sharon Hodde Miller, author of *Nice*

"Let's be real: friendships can be funky! Our friend-guide Andi walks us through the healing process to get from hurting to healthy boundaries in all our relationships. Not only does Andi write about friendships, she is a great friend who lives out these words with conviction."

Bianca Juarez Olthoff, pastor, teacher, and bestselling author of *How to Have Your Life Not Suck*

"All the wounds we all carry and skewed perceptions we have of what our relationships could and should be like can get 'complicated.' In Andi's book *Friendship—It's Complicated*, she masterfully taps into our basic human need for connection and authenticity and challenges us to be the friends we are looking to have. Andi teaches us what it practically looks like to face our past wounds and take extreme ownership of the part we play in our own fulfillment and happiness in our relationships. She inspires us to get honest about cycles and belief systems that keep us bound in dysfunction, isolation, and loneliness, which is the opposite of God's original intent for our lives. Andi gives us hope that we can heal, rebuild, restore, and create a new way of connecting with ourselves and others in a healthy way. By taking this journey with her, you will be sure to experience something new, fresh, and life-giving in your friendships no matter your age or season of life."

Irene Rollins, pastor, speaker, author, and recovery activist

"All I can say is 'WOW!' I could not put this book down, simply because I've never read a book like it before. The honesty combined with transparency, vulnerability, and raw emotion bleeds through every page and will absolutely pierce through the deepest recesses of your soul. Andi's journey is our journey in one way, shape, or form, yet God has seen fit to anoint her so that through her personal experience, she has been able to brilliantly tackle this very complex issue and thus propel us to courageously venture out of our caves of self-pity, face our fears, and take on the challenge once again to have genuine friendships, which are so desperately needed in all our lives. This book is for every woman!"

Maria Durso, copastor, Overseer Saints Church

"It's not easy finding friends who are for you and who want to build with you. I'm so grateful that Andi is addressing this topic on friendships. Many friendships are fake, and you can often tell from the moment you meet someone if they are interested in forming a relationship with you or if they are using you to their advantage. How do we learn to take risks in building friendships that could be the real deal and that will last a lifetime? Through Andi's experiences, she reveals truths about why we need to first become a better friend if we desire more authentic friendships."

Lisa Kai, senior pastor, Inspire Church

"Once again, Andi delivers a helpful, honest resource for women. Friendship is a lifeline, but wounds from the past, like rejection, betrayal, comparison, and insecurity, hinder authentic connections with others. Through storytelling, Scripture, and humor, Andi will help you reflect, recover, and heal so that you can experience meaningful, reciprocal relationships with others."

Ashley Abercrombie, author of *Rise of the Truth Teller* and *Love Is the Resistance*, cohost of the *Why Tho* Podcast

"I am not exaggerating when I say I ugly cried like a '90s Claire Danes as I read these pages. I am also not exaggerating when I say Andi Andrew lives and breathes every bit of this book and its subject matter. So, get ready; you're about to sit through a clinic on friendship, overcoming, and how to see and love people. If you allow Andi's words and wisdom to wash over you, you'll leave these pages changed. I know this firsthand because I did."

Chari Orozco, author, speaker, showrunner at AWKNG+TV

FRIENDSHIP

it's complicated

Avoid the Drama,
Create Authentic Connection,
and Fulfill Your Purpose Together

ANDI ANDREW

BakerBooks

a division of Baker Publishing Group
Grand Rapids, Michigan

© 2021 by Andi Andrew

Published by Baker Books
a division of Baker Publishing Group
PO Box 6287, Grand Rapids, MI 49516-6287
www.bakerbooks.com

Printed in the United States of America

Library of Congress Cataloging-in-Publication Data
Names: Andrew, Andi, 1978– author.
Title: Friendship—it's complicated : avoid the drama, create authentic connection, and fulfill your purpose together / Andi Andrew.
Description: Grand Rapids, Michigan : Baker Books, a division of Baker Publishing Group, [2021] | Includes bibliographical references.
Identifiers: LCCN 2021003783 | ISBN 9780801094316 (paperback) | ISBN 9781540901897 (casebound) | ISBN 9781493432820 (ebook)
Subjects: LCSH: Female friendship—Religious aspects—Christianity. | Christian women—Religious life.
Classification: LCC BV4647.F7 A56 2021 | DDC 241/.6762082—dc23
LC record available at https://lccn.loc.gov/2021003783

The author is represented by the Christopher Ferebee Agency, www.christopher ferebee.com.

Baker Publishing Group publications use paper produced from sustainable forestry practices and post-consumer waste whenever possible.

21 22 23 24 25 26 27   7 6 5 4 3 2 1

To my beautiful mother, Mavis:
We fought hard for this.
Thank you for being committed
to genuine connection and reconciliation,
no matter how painful, no matter the cost.
You have taught me never to give up.

To all the women out there
longing for genuine friendship:
Don't lose heart. It's worth the fight.

contents

letter to the reader

Sister, friend, fellow woman longing to uncomplicate friendship,

I have come to the conclusion that relationships inform us *and* form us. And friendships of the female kind are in a league of their own.

Personally, believing I could even get to a place where I'd feel confident enough to write a book about friendship has been a long and winding road. I mean, are we ever really "there"? Maybe. Maybe not. Am I an expert? Far from it. I am *completely* imperfect in friendships and have learned much more than I'd like to admit through innumerable mistakes, gut-wrenching pain, heartache, betrayal, comparison, insecurity, fear, gossip, isolation, rejection, and drama. And, *thank God*, I have also learned from friends who have stuck around through the years (and, yes, *my* own personal drama). They've given me more grace and unceasing love than I've ever deserved, and their persistence and patience have healed me.

I've walked through *a lot* in friendships, good and bad, and since you're holding this book in your hands, I'm sure you have too. Truth be told, I have had to walk away from some friendships for the right reasons, because ending them was necessary for my physical, mental, and emotional health. Other times, I've walked away for the wrong reasons: out of insecurity and fear—avoiding making peace because it required humility, conflict, and hard conversations. I've been way too good (like, Olympian-level good) at self-preservation in friendships. I've looked the part, acting like I was all in when *really*, I was withholding because I was afraid of being taken advantage of or having to carry all the responsibility to build the friendship. I was afraid of being made the fool or abandoned—*again*—playing the "victim" card in another relationship gone wrong. I've believed so many lies about female friendships that I've been close to doing away with them altogether. I mean, I have a husband and four kids—that's enough relationship for a lifetime, right? Nope. For me, that's an excuse to hide and not try. I've learned that as I lean in to the kindness and love of God, I simply can't get away with being the victim. I am loved and empowered to grow, change, and walk in grace and humility as I choose to dive back into relationship, often with the growth of thicker skin and a heart made more tender.

I've had a deep longing ever since I can remember, even as a child, to have female friends who were safe, forgiving, full of grace, and able to deliver the truth in love without abandoning me once they saw the real, imperfect, nonperforming me. I've longed for a freedom in friendship where I can vulnerably be myself without that vulnerability being twisted, taken advantage of, or used against me—and I'm sure you have too. Let's be honest, I've needed to *be* that friend and reciprocate all these things to others who have chosen to draw close to me, and I haven't always done it well. But I have learned. I have grown. And I have changed—and I am still changing. Have you desired to have friends that you could completely let your guard down with? Relationships in which competition isn't even an option because everyone knows their worth, and drama is saved for the stages of Broadway?

The hard truth is, women can cause acute pain to one another that's different from the pain men can cause in our lives. I believe it's *so* painful because somewhere deep down, we know that we are meant to nurture one another, have each other's backs, and appreciate and champion our diversity while cheering each other on. When we're pitted against one another and begin contending for our place, we replace comradery and solidarity with pride, competition, or being right no matter the cost, breaking our sacred connection as women. When this happens, I think we're somehow aware on a cellular level that something's just not right. We *are* better together, and not just when we wear it on a T-shirt but when we actively live it. Yet sometimes we just don't know how to do "together" well. My sincere hope and prayer is that this book helps to nudge you forward, even if it's just a few steps in the right direction.

If we each take a few minutes and reflect candidly, we'll realize we've all faced rejection from other women—every last one of us. We've all had mothers, daughters, sisters, aunts, teachers, female leaders, pastors, mentors, bosses, or friends that we've chosen to be vulnerable with. We've allowed them into sacred places in our hearts only to be hurt or rejected in some way, shape, or form. Then it's probable that we've said in our hearts or declared with our mouths, "I thought we were friends," while slowly backing away from the relationship. The result of this pain can cause us to run to God, receive healing, and continue to build relationships, or it can cause us to make unhealthy vows, stating, "Never again will I let another woman hurt me," choosing isolation over comradery and connection.

I genuinely believe that we all want friendships in which we can avoid the drama, create authentic connection, and fulfill our purpose—*together*—right? But doesn't this sort of friendship seem like a unicorn standing next to a pot of gold at the rainbow's end in a mystical land? I can honestly say that I have some unicorns in my life, but they have not come without time and intentionality. So, sister, friend, fellow woman in the friendship wrestle, this book is an active book that will cause you to face yourself, untangle the mess you may find yourself in, repent, and surrender your heart openly before the Lord so that you can walk in freedom. This book will cause you to want to champion others and, in turn, to fulfill your purpose with your sisters.

I'm going to shed some light on my mistakes and the ugliness I have brought into friendship. I'm not throwing anyone under the bus here; I'm taking responsibility for my own life, and I hope you will too. I will share some of how God has walked me through different moments and seasons, illuminating the truth to me and in turn setting me free. I will share how He continually and tenderly leads me to take ownership for my heart and life, instructing me along the way with His wisdom on how to do friendship better with each passing year.

My greatest desire is that you'll humbly allow God to lead you to truth, bring healing, and pour out wisdom as you walk into new territory on your own friendship journey. Dare I suggest you choose to go through this book with a group of women? You never know, one of your closest, forever friends may be in that group. Hey, even if you're scared out of your mind to be vulnerable with them, can I encourage you to tell the truth and own your story anyway? I pray that together you'll find great healing, encouragement, revelation, life, connection, and freedom in these pages.

So, let us begin.

All my love,

Andi

part 1

FACING YOURSELF

chapter 1

THE WOMAN WOUND

When we have gotten negative mothering, we can begin
a pattern of mistrusting for the rest of our lives. We
hide our needs and vulnerability. We become combative
and aggressive. To show that we can't be controlled, we
control others.

Dr. Henry Cloud and Dr. John Townsend

I remember my first woman wound. Do you?

Well, she wasn't a woman at all but my five-year-old best
friend whom I'd met on the first day of kindergarten. She meant
no harm whatsoever; she simply communicated kindly that she
wanted to play with another friend at recess instead of me, *yet*
the tangible ache in my chest, ringing in my ears, and tingling
in my limbs signaled fresh rejection to my brain, causing me
to cry uncontrollably. My response, in hindsight, seems like a
gross overreaction, but then again, I was five. I remember lying
facedown on the grass, still wet with dew, as the sun shone

through the small tent I'd made over my head with my arms to cover the embarrassment of my tears. She kept gently touching my back, letting me know that we were still best friends and that she just wanted to play with someone else at recess that day. She was soft and tender, but I was devastated. The rejection hit me deep. No matter how I pleaded, I couldn't get her to play with me, and that scared five-year-old me.

I hate to say it, but as a grown woman, sometimes I still feel that little-woman wound turn like a knife in my skin when I perceive the possibility of a fresh rejection from a friend or sense my inability to control the state of a relationship. That dull ache in my chest returns, along with the awareness that my limbs sting with the sensation of pins and needles, accompanied by a slight loss of sound around me like I've gone underwater for a moment. One of my greatest fears is that I'll be inadequate in a relationship. That I'll never be enough and therefore will be emotionally cut off from those I love without knowing why or what I have done, and that I won't have the option to be let back in to heal and restore things. This loss of perceived control keeps me from being vulnerable. It keeps me from connecting. It keeps me choosing isolation because it seems like the safer option.

The Mom Factor

We often talk about the father wound, but what about the mother wound? As a mother, I am keenly aware that I am a primary sculptor of my children's patterns of thinking, attachment, connection, ability to nurture, and so much more. The mother wound, or woman wound, is something we need to look at to help us get to a place where we can make greater authentic connection in our friendships and relationships.

The truth is, my first woman wound came from the first woman who ever had the power to hurt me—my mother. Now, before you wonder, yes, I *have* talked to my mom extensively about the words on these pages, and she has given me freedom to write about our relationship *because* we are committed to continually walking in healing—together—turning to each other, and fighting for connection, whatever the cost. And I realize that this may *not* be the case for many of you.

Maybe you have a great relationship with your mother and have always been able to connect with other women easily— this is a gift that truly needs to be shared—but I also recognize that it doesn't mean you haven't experienced a wound or wounds from other women in your life. On the other hand, you may walk in brokenness with your mother and have a legitimate need to have firm boundaries in place with her relationally. It's possible that you may not know how to make a move with your mother because you want her to make the first move. It can be complicated, I know.

Our mothers greatly shape our world. Remember, *our relationships inform us and form us,* so just take a second before we go further and consider how your relationship with your mom, or lack thereof, affected your life as a child. How has her mothering affected you as an adult? There is no right or wrong answer here, just self-awareness that it could be affecting your relationships with other women in the present.

Dr. Henry Cloud and Dr. John Townsend say in their book *The Mom Factor,* "We need to look at the patterns that we learned in our relationship with our mother. Patterns of avoidance, control, compliance, dominance, passivity, aggressiveness and overcontrol, mistrust and a host of others can get hardwired into our brains. We were made to take in those patterns and to live by them. That is what parenting is about. We internalize the ways of our parents, and then live by them."[1]

I am hyperaware of my shortfalls as a mother, and this awareness has given me grace upon grace for my own mom. So, let me honor her here for a moment. Mama Mavis is a fighter. An overcomer and a lover. Her story is one of tragedy and triumph. She is living proof that Jesus is real, alive, active, and working on her behalf. She is truly thriving in the face of an enemy that has come to take her out, time and time again, since she inhaled her first breath. Without her, I personally wouldn't still be here. She has jumped into the pit of the darkest nights of my soul when I was genuinely done. Done with ministry, done with marriage, done with people, and done with life. She has had the right words to speak, prophetic words to minister to my spirit, powerful prayers to pray, and unconditional love to pour out when I couldn't see clearly, when I didn't know what to do. But our relationship has not always been this way.

As I started to write this book, I kept getting stuck. I knew I had to write about my relationship with my mother in a vulnerable way, but I didn't want to dishonor her in the process, nor did I want to blame her for my issues. Yes, some patterns of my behavior and thinking have come from attachment-related issues that stem back to her, which I have had therapy for. I also take responsibility now, as an adult who is alive in Christ, to consistently seek transformation to walk in wholeness, be it through relational accountability to a small circle of friends, therapy, prayer, meditation on the Word, or having a flexible yet strategic game plan for my mental, emotional, and spiritual health throughout each shifting season. My mom cannot always be the target of my aggression, anger, or blame, nor my excuse for why I can't seem to uncomplicate certain friendships. Cloud and Townsend say, "As you begin to see and understand the missing elements in the mothering you received, your responsibility is to grieve and forgive so that way you may be healed of whatever your mother might have done wrong."[2] There is purpose in why we visit some places in our past, not to pitch a tent and live there but to bring Jesus, the Healer, in with us that we may be made whole and move forward.

So, how did I get unstuck and start telling the truth in these pages? Well, breakthrough never happens the way we think it will. Here's how the dam burst and the flow of words began to spill out of my heart.

A very close friend iced me out for, what seemed to me, no particular reason. I was traveling to the state where she lived and was excited to get some time with her. Knowing I wanted to see her, my friend chose to purchase tickets for a trip out of her home state the day before I arrived, even though she had the option to leave the day after I arrived. (FYI, this friend and I are good now and have talked through all of this.) When she told me the news (via text) that she was leaving the day before I would get there, I spiraled—like, started crying like five-year-old Andi in the schoolyard sort of spiral—wondering what I had done so wrong that she wouldn't want to see me when I was making an intentional effort to connect. Had I offended or hurt her and she hadn't told me why? Did she have a deep-seated issue with me? Did she just not like me but had never told me?

I called my mom immediately to talk it through with her. Her peaceful tone helped stop my thoughts from wildly pinging all over the place. She assured me that even if this friend did have an issue with me, it wasn't for me to fix or carry, *and* it wasn't healthy for me to make assumptions if my friend had never voiced any problems. And this is where the break-through came . . .

I sat there, silently pondering her words, and then it hit me. "Mom, whenever something goes wrong with another woman in my life—friend, leader, staff member, or peer—I always assume the position of taking complete responsibility for the problem. I'll even let them tell me it's all my fault when it's clearly not. I carry this massive weight on my shoulders, like I could've done something more, said something more, been something more, but I'm never enough. I always come up short. I don't know how to connect with women in a healthy way. And, Mom, can I say something hard?" My mom nodded lovingly over FaceTime, so I went on. "You know I've forgiven you and I love you, but I think it comes from you. From when I was so young and you'd share things with me, things that really only an adult or counselor could've helped you with, things that were so heavy for me as a little girl and teenager to carry that I felt like I wasn't enough. That I didn't love you well enough or help you enough or do or say what you needed, because I was a child. I was ill-equipped to help you in your pain. I feel like I became your emotional mother—like we switched roles, and I wasn't very good at it."

At this point, I was holding back from hysterically crying just to get these honest words out. I was aware of how my heart felt in that moment: it was aching in my chest, and my throat was tight with hesitation as I swallowed hard to hold back the desire to sob uncontrollably. If I'm honest, somewhere in my subconscious, I was bracing for a manipulative "I'm sorry," where she would cry, and then I'd feel bad for her and internally assume a position of responsibility for the emotional strength of our relationship. I mean, she hadn't done that with me in years, but this fresh wound from a friend put me on guard, opening up a door to old trauma while shedding light on a well-worn belief system in me. I've learned through my Celebrate Recovery Step Study group that we all have "hurts, hang-ups, and habits," and in a split second of conversation with my mom, my past hurts and present hang-ups came erupting to the surface.

And then my mom said the most healing words: "Andi, you're right. I was boundaryless and I hurt you. Will you forgive me?"

I was stunned. Complete ownership. No manipulation. No crocodile tears. No "I'm sorry you felt that way." She didn't make the conversation about her or how hard her circumstances were at the time; she just owned it, asked for forgiveness, and made amends.

Oh, and friend, healing came like a flood.

The dam broke and I began to wail—like, the neighbors would hear and might even call the cops sort of wail. Decades of belief systems that crippled me in relationships with women hit the floor and shattered like glass. And they were swept away in the tender love of Jesus. I think it's important to say here that this moment did not instantly fix nor make all things right in my other relationships, but it did firmly establish that a new work had begun. A new layer of healing was emerging for me to now steward and walk in.

I said, "Mom, I want to write about us, but I don't want to dishonor you. I love you and we've worked so hard to have a safe relationship."

She just smiled and said, "I trust you. Write whatever you want. It's a story of redemption."

So, you have a promise from me (with my mama's permission) that I won't hold back in these pages. I will be vulnerable and honest, threading everything with the truth of Jesus's redeeming love, encouraging you along the way with actionable steps and points of self-reflection.

As we lean in together, let's go back to move forward.

The truth is, even if you are in a good place with your mom, it's probable that your relationship with her still informs you to this day on how to relate to other women. For instance, because my mom leaned on me emotionally from a young age and even into adulthood, I unconsciously assumed a motherly position toward her. We had a codependent relationship that began to transfer over to my friendships. Codependency is "a state of mutual dependence between two people, especially when one partner relies emotionally on supporting and caring for the other partner."[3] I started to notice the same unconscious cycle in myself when women got close to me and had any sort of heavy emotional needs. My walls would slowly go up because their needs were too much for me. I had been there and done that, and it was too hard. I was ill-equipped to carry them and their problems. I also discovered that I had an underlying assumption that I needed to carry their burdens for them, even if they never asked me to. I was boundaryless and bent toward codependency because that is what I learned growing up.

I also noticed that I'd too quickly dive deep into relationships with new friends, giving of myself and sharing with intense vulnerability on the first or second "friend date," because deep down I was so desperate for someone to be there for *me* emotionally. I had no idea how to *share* burdens with one another; I just wanted someone to carry mine *for* me because it was such a profound unmet need. It was like every time I sat down with a new prospective friend, I thought, *This may be the one.* But the moment a friendship turned because I deemed it unsafe in any way (from my broken perspective), I'd emotionally exit and slowly back away.

Now, we all have unmet needs from childhood because we all have imperfect, human parents. In adulthood, we have to become aware of how we are trying to meet those needs in healthy or unhealthy ways.

Our Response to the Woman Wound

In the quote that opened this chapter, Cloud and Townsend help us to understand that negative mothering can affect how we think, feel, and act toward others in relationship.

For me, control was and *can still be* a first response to any woman wound I receive. If you hurt me, I may choose to isolate, put up walls, and walk away, denying you access to my heart.

When I looked through the harsh lens of bitterness and unforgiveness, I saw my mother as an adulterer and a manipulator, *but* at the same time, she would have died for any of her four kids (and still would). As I grew, in age and maturity, I asked more questions and realized that she was devastatingly abused throughout her entire life (including during my childhood, though not by my father—ever), and insecurity paired with manipulation became her weapon of safety and control. With compassion, I can clearly see the trauma and pain she faced and her response to it—right or wrong—for what it was. Yet, it doesn't change the fact that it created a strange environment to grow up in. Hers was an extreme "I would die for you" sort of love, accompanied by insecurity and manipulation. And even though I didn't know everything about my upbringing and my parents' brokenness (because it wasn't just my mom's but my dad's brokenness too) until I started digging up the past when I was nineteen.

When I *did* find out the truth of my parents' sin while I was under their roof, in my spiritual, newly born-again pride at nineteen years of age, I decided to ice my mother out of my life for seven years until I got pregnant with my firstborn, and the Holy Spirit asked me, "Would you want your children to treat you the way you're treating your mother?" (You can read my first book, *She Is Free*, specifically chapter 4, "Freedom from Unforgiveness," for the extended version of that story.) And my quick, repentant, fear-of-God answer was, "No!"

When I put all the pieces together, everything from my upbringing finally made sense. Yes, I'd see my mom for holidays and visits, but she knew she wasn't welcome into my heart, and I had good reasons for it, until my unforgiveness slowly tortured me like it did the unmerciful servant in Matthew 18:21–35. I wanted forgiveness from the King for my own sin but refused to give it to those who had hurt me. The bitterness was breaking me down.

The initial breakthrough and desire to rebuild came when I was a week away from giving birth. My mom came into town to be my birth doula (since she is a birth and postpartum doula professionally, and I had pictured her there beside me since I was a little girl). As we sat in the nursery, folding baby clothes, with the warm sun shining through the windows of our little townhouse on that brisk winter day in Sydney, I asked for her forgiveness for my hypocrisy and pharisaical ways. And without hesitation, she let me into her heart, and I let her back into mine. Every year since then, we have walked out a steady journey of reconciliation, working intentionally to recover that which was lost. And our God, as per usual, has been nothing but present and good through it all.

I wanted my mother, Mavis, to share from her perspective all that God has done. Though she could fill a whole book of her own, and probably should, here are some words of life from her heart to yours to celebrate the testimony of Jesus.

From My Mama's Heart, in Her Words

It's amazing that our children have become such giants of forgiveness and love.

I especially believe this because I definitely gave them plenty to work with in the forgiveness department. This is not to excuse myself in the slightest, but what parent can look back and say, "Well done. Goodness! I was a perfect parent!"? Not one of us.

Beyond the specific details of parenting by emotion, I am healed enough in my own life now to own the actual tragic mistakes and sins of wanting to be a great friend with my children instead of being a rock and protector, a teacher and moral guide, an example that made them proud, exemplifying the love of Christ in integrity from the core of my being. Oh, I *loved* my children, *that* is for certain. The sun still rises and sets on them, and there is simply nothing else in my life more treasured than them and my marriage. Maybe I have, more than most, seen the result of "Love covering a multitude of sins."

Giant mistake—using my daughters as sounding boards and even healers, counselors, and a place to unload my worries and concerns. How could I? How did I not see this would make for children who grew up feeling that love meant you had to take responsibility for someone (everyone) else even though you couldn't do a *thing* to make it better. Seeing the pain I brought into their lives was devastating. But what would be more devastating would be to believe they (and I) would have to accept it and just live with it forever. I am so glad that this is not so.

It's very important here to share that I couldn't admit this for quite a long time. Being riddled with guilt isn't a cure to make a better relationship with the ones I hurt. That only prolongs "the crazy" and separates us, but experiencing and knowing God's love and forgiveness have given me not only my own identity but also the desire to unpack and unload burdens that were never meant to belong to others in my life but that I loaded upon them. Specifically here, I am speaking of Andi. To say I am responsible and to reconcile to the core with her was always a dream, but I felt so bad when we'd talk about it at times in the past that I'd shrink back into my insecure shell and make it hard for her to even ask questions or bare her heart to me. Extraordinary pressure and anxiety don't begin to explain how we each felt as we tried and seemed to fail along the way. But we kept trying and kept seeing God do miracles.

I am aware of the pain I caused. No hiding that. But now I *own* it. It's not pretty. But the miracle is, now that I own it, I also own the complete forgiveness I have been given as a gift. The walls of feeling and acting insecure when confronted are destroyed and powerless. So much so that now I'm excited and courageous as we take down the old lies. I see the damage they did in my beautiful daughter, and it's not right or fair. It never was—but she honored me and spoke well of me. God blesses her and all our children for that. They are champions.

Back to the specific brokenness between Andi and me: to declare freedom over her, come into agreement with her, and have the honor through the unmistakable power of God to remove burdens that were never hers to carry is inexplicable. For her to be able to love by removing the old lies and burdens I actually placed on her is miraculous and incredibly empowering and beautiful. We've done this through prayer, through tough conversations, through tears and laughter. The truth is, I have the unique authority and responsibility to do so in the love of Christ as her mother and as the one who put that burden there in the first place! He's shown me my dark places and given me a new life by loving me even in and through that darkness.

So, there is no fear in me from being wrong or making mistakes. There *is* remorse and sadness, yes. But that is also healed by Jesus's love. Now it's time to set things in order. He's healed me, and now I love to take my old insecurity and blaming and fear and vicarious living through the innocence and successes of my children and set them in plain sight so that I can ask for forgiveness. I have chosen to stand up and tell Satan and his demonic attacks and lies to be banished from my life and my children's and their children's and their children's.

Walking in Truth and Freedom

Once we begin to understand or discern a truth about ourselves and our formative relationships with those closest to us, we can start to take steps that will embolden us to begin to make different choices. We can put things into perspective, seeing why we do the things we do, without condemning ourselves but instead empowering ourselves to embark on a path to do the work and change.

Take a moment to consider and reflect on the type of mothering you received. Was your mom the hovering, "I will never leave you alone" kind? The controlling, "I know what's best for you and will make all your decisions" kind? The "I will pay all your bills and buy you all the things so you know I love you but don't have emotional energy for you" kind? Was your mom the victim of all her circumstances, and you were her listening ear? Was your mom never there for you when you really needed her? Was your mom the kind who put you on a pedestal and made you feel like you couldn't fail? Was she the "You're too emotional and too much, and you shouldn't feel that way" kind of mother? Was she the kind who kept up appearances, but behind closed doors everything was falling apart? Maybe she denied your reality (and possibly her own), so she wasn't there for you. Was she the military, "Don't mess up," "Don't show your emotions" kind? Maybe she couldn't regulate her emotions, and her anger was scary for you. Was she the "Why can't you just be more like . . ." kind? Was she the abusive, fear-monger kind? Or maybe she simply didn't understand you, or she physically abandoned you. It's also possible that you never had the chance to meet her due to her passing away when you were young or some other tragic circumstance.

Whatever your relationship has been or presently is with your mother, it's so empowering to know that you can heal. There is hope. You can grow, change, forgive, grieve, let go, and move forward *in uncomplicated friendship* with other women who embrace you in all your imperfection.

With that said, before we move on, let's stop for a few moments together so we can reflect, become aware, and begin to initiate healing, forgiveness, and freedom in our lives. Through-out each chapter, we will take moments to be still and reflect. Sometimes in the middle of a chapter, because that's where it makes the most sense to pause, and other times at the end of a chapter. I hope these Reflection Points motivate movement toward growth and wholeness.

REFLECTION POINTS

- Do you remember your first woman wound? How has that affected you in friendship today? Take a moment to discuss with the group, if you're gathering with one, or simply write it down to process on your own.
- What lies have you believed because of that wound?
- Take a moment in silence and invite the Holy Spirit in to speak to you. Ask what God wants to replace that lie with to heal the wound. In your own words, speak the truth out loud to receive love and healing.

- What elements of mothering have gaps missing for
  you? Remember, these things are good to identify, not
  so you can sling shame and blame but so you can begin
  to grieve, forgive, and receive healing from whatever
  your mother may have done, or not done, that brought
  pain. Consider setting some time aside to do just that:
  grieve, walk through prayers of forgiveness, worship,
  and receive God's love and healing.

- How has your relationship with your mom informed
  you, in good ways or bad, as to how you relate and
  connect in female friendship? What steps can you
  take to break any unhealthy cycles you are possibly
  becoming aware of? Maybe you could join a faith community, a recovery group, a discipleship group, or a
  book study, or find a great therapist. Maybe you could
  bravely share this with a friend or confidant. This is
  by no means an extensive list but simple examples to
  get you thinking toward an action plan to break cycles
  and create new rhythms in your own life.

chapter 2

ON THE OUTSIDE
LOOKING IN

I know what it's like when the things you believe make
you feel like you're on the outside looking in.

Jodi Picoult

I was nervous—like, run-to-the-bathroom-every-five-minutes
nervous.

I had been invited to an intimate luncheon at the Plaza
Hotel of all places with ten other women who were doing great
things in the city, and I was more nervous than I remember
being for a long time. Why was the potential of making a new
girlfriend or group of girlfriends so intense? Why was anxiety
mounting at neck-rash levels and the desire to perform ever so
slightly rising up, all while the need to put on my imaginary
suit of "Don't get too close, though" armor was coming upon
me like a flock of hungry seagulls?

Pull it together, sister. You're an adult. Breathe.

I wore an outfit I thought was Plaza-worthy, only to walk out the door of my house and realize, while running to the subway after the "get the four kids out the door flurry," that my tailor had hemmed my Free People jumpsuit too short (insert shocked, angry, and embarrassed emojis here). I was already late for work, so high-waters (not cool high-waters) would be the outfit of the day, and I'd have to work it like I did it on purpose. Because, you know, I wasn't already trying to overcome some unidentified insecurity gnawing at my soul. Thank God, my hair was on point—naturally curly hair for the win—and I actually did my makeup, like, all of it. I am a barefaced bandit most of the time, showing up at school to pick up my kids looking like I forgot where the shower was in my house.

I casually walked into the Plaza like I went there all the time and saw that I was the first to arrive. Good thing I knew the host, so it wasn't awkward. We connected and caught up. Then as people began to arrive, we all started talking about the usual getting-to-know-you things. What's your name? What do you do? How long have you been in the city? How many kids? You know, all those things. Then our host asked us to go around the table and individually share. It was my turn first. I didn't know how much to divulge, and I wanted to keep it short and not steal time from others, so that's just what I did. But then, as every other woman went, they shared more and more, baring their souls with vulnerability and honesty. I was kicking myself, thinking I should've given more, said more, *been* more. Lies began to nudge me, trying to make their way into my heart. Lies like, *You don't belong at this table. Andi, how are you even going to connect with these women? Will they even like you? At first they might, but then they'll probably leave like the rest . . .*

My goodness! What am I? Five years old, about to start kindergarten?

It sure felt like it.

As each woman shared, I became more and more insecure, amazed at their lives, their gifts, and the good work they were doing in the city. I felt like I was on the outside looking in at a beautiful world that I desperately wanted to enter into, but I wasn't sure if I would ever belong. At the same time, my phone was blowing up, distracting me from fully connecting. Urgent work things back at the office, then messages that my youngest son had a fever spiking at 104, so I needed to leave early and rush home to him. Whew. I had a legitimate out. I was going to reject these women before they rejected me, and they didn't even know it.

On my commute home, I pondered my thought process and searched the areas of my heart that still needed healing and freedom, specifically the area of friendship with women. How had I gotten to a place where I believed the lie that I was on the outside looking in? Ultimately, it was because of unhealed pain. It was subconscious, but it was there, lingering, trying to pull me away from building authentic relationships.

I had been through a five-year stretch of broken friendships. Some of them had been fully restored, and some still had open loops that I've had to accept may never close. I had walked through love, loss, and grief in relationships with other women, which made me gun-shy. I had actively gone after healing in my heart, but to purposefully enter into new relationships that hadn't been tested by the fire of trial and time with a small collective of women who want to build something together and who actually live in my city and aren't going anywhere scared the living daylights out of me.

35

Each and every one of us is beautifully unique and comes to the table of friendship with our own unspoken expectations, brokenness, and genuine unmet needs. And the great thing is that we are created by God, wired with the ability to change as we lean in to His goodness and know ourselves more intimately before Him and in Him. Self-awareness is a huge factor in the ability to transform and stop blaming others for why we are where we are. As we continually submit our whole lives, repent of our sins and partnerships with fear, and choose to step into love, we will break up with drama in our lives and have the ability to establish genuine connection with others. In turn, we will be fulfilling our purpose—together—with other amazing women.

REFLECTION POINTS

- Take a moment and ask yourself what causes you to put yourself on the outside looking in. Fear? Unhealed pain? Insecurity? Shyness? Maybe you're an introvert and find it hard to dive in to new relationships. What lies have you possibly believed?
- What is one thing you can surrender to God or repent of to receive healing and truth from Him? Begin to declare and affirm that truth out loud.
- Take a moment and confess your sins that have caused you to be separated from others.

  If we confess our sins, he is faithful and just and will forgive us our sins and purify us from all unrighteousness. (1 John 1:9)

Know Yourself

I've been learning about the Enneagram (insert eye roll) because for the past few years, everyone has been asking me, "What number are you?" and I'm like, "I don't actually care. You can't box me in. I'm not a number; I'm a human being. Hey, friends, stop asking me this question." I give a million variations of the same line, avoiding yet another personality test that tells me all my faults or "who I am," when I'm an individual who can't be put in a box.

So, after years, I took the official Enneagram test and found out that my top four numbers are Four, Nine, Eight, and Three. The Four and the Nine came in as a tie for first place, and the Eight and the Three came in a few points below the others as a secondary tie. So I went down the Enneagram rabbit hole, reading all the books (*The Road Back to You* by Ian Morgan Cron and Suzanne Stabile did it for me), and came to the conclusion that I am as complicated and annoying, self-centered and emotional as I thought I was, and I didn't need a test to tell me that. I am a Four with a Three wing. A Romantic Individualist (the Four) Successful Achiever (the Three). Did you get that? A Romantic, Individualist, Successful, Achiever. Laugh with me, please. So that I don't cry. Beth McCord, an Enneagram coach who wrote a series of books on each Enneagram type, writes this about how Fours typically communicate: "When I'm doing well, I am authentic, deep, empathetic, a great listener when others are sad or grieving, and I express my emotions with inner balance. When I am not doing well, I can be moody, emotionally intense and explosive, cold and detached, condescending, and steer the conversation to focus on me."[1] Yikes! All 100 percent true.

So, I am "emo" with a knack to perform and get things done when needed—while making sure you think I look good while I do them. Oh, and when it comes to relationships, don't even bother. I will never be good enough for you— trust me. I'm deeply in touch with where I'm at, and if you scratch the surface, watch out. It's complicated. No wait—I am complicated.

And, trust me, if you get complicated or too needy—you're out too. Pray for my husband and any girlfriend who has remained close to me for over five years. I mean it.

If you meet me at work or wherever I'm getting a job done, you're going see the Three—my Achiever. You'll even see it in how I run my house. Pray for my kids. They hate organizing things. Except for my daughter—oh how she blesses me with her attention to detail. When I ask my boys to organize and clean their room with the systems I've so lovingly put in place, they nod and smile with a distant look in their eyes as if they're far, far away in the prehistoric era thinking about velociraptors.

If you see me communicating in a public setting or if you read any of my books, you'll see a mishmash of my Four and Three—the push and pull of my being deeply in touch with my feelings and the heart of God while desperately wanting to make sure you clearly hear His voice, know His Word, and, first and foremost, stay connected to Him. The Three helps me push past any melancholy that may manifest in my genuine desire to run away and live on a farm, isolated from society, for the rest of my life. Away from the mess of humanity that Jesus came to save and that He keeps asking me to love and pour my life out for. Yes, it's so dramatic over here. Did I mention you should pray for my husband? Now would be a good time to start.

Let me say this: the Enneagram is not the be-all, end-all; it's just a helpful tool on a journey of self-discovery and understanding, because the truth is, if we don't know who we are and what we are potentially bringing to the table in friendship—in any relationship for that matter—it can harm our connection instead of fostering it. We are all fearfully and wonderfully made; it's simply a fact. God adores who you are—He intentionally made you—and wants to heal any brokenness that has the potential to build barriers to genuine connection. On a daily basis, we need the saving grace and mercy that Jesus brings into our lives—we cannot save ourselves without Him, nor can we become more like Him on our own. If we try to do this life without Jesus, we begin to operate from a position of self-help instead of surrender, and we find ourselves in similar broken cycles instead of being formed more into the likeness of Christ—which is the goal.

It's also important that we think about how our female relational history comes into play with regard to openly being ourselves in friendship. I mean, we all have a mother; otherwise we wouldn't exist. But remember the woman wound that we've already addressed? This is in the mix as we step into friendship. Take stock again: What was that relationship like? Was it picture-perfect or fraught with strife? Was it cordial and cold, void of emotion or connection? Or was it steeped in deep love and good memories, albeit imperfect? Maybe it had jealousy and competition at its core, void of nurture. Or possibly abandonment—the ultimate betrayal of a mother-daughter relationship—rejection at a deep level that brings about a mistrust of women in general.

Before we are born, we're created to be literally bonded to our mothers, first with an umbilical cord while in utero and then through breastfeeding after we are born into this world.

Breastfeeding stimulates the release of oxytocin, sometimes called the "love hormone," in the mother's and the baby's brains, fostering love, nurturing, and an unspeakable emotional bond between mother and child. These things aid in building a healthy attachment, and that's just the physiological side of it. We all know I'm not a scientist, but I do have common sense—mothers and their children are connected in more ways than one. In my own household, both my husband and I can be home, even sitting next to each other, and the kids will only ask me questions, will need me to do things for them, and will interrupt me when I'm trying to do something I enjoy, like putting my feet up at the end of a long day to read a good novel with the door closed to my bedroom. If I put up a boundary, they'll sure as heck put their toe right on it or try to breach the physical door to my room with something very "urgent," at least in their minds. I've learned through years of experience, that it's in our children's nature to connect, bond, and need us. So, when certain needs were not met by our mothers (all mothers fall short, true?), or attachments weren't made or were severed, involving some form of trauma or distress, naturally there is a void within us. Then unmet needs and unspoken expectations tend to echo out from our lives, touching those around us.

It's good to remember that in any relationship, we all bring our family-of-origin perspectives, which give us an understanding of how to relate to others. We come in with narratives that shape us and perspectives that inform us and also form our world and relational view. We don't come alone; we bring all the things.

So, as I mentioned in chapter 1, operating in a broken and dysfunctional relationship with my mom when I was growing up resulted in attachment-related trauma that informed me regarding the safety or lack of safety I could expect in relationships with women. I have sought counseling and prayer around this, and I jump back into them when needed. They have helped me to become present in my friendships and to recognize when the residue of past issues with my mom becomes the dysfunctional root of my pulling close and then pushing away women in my life. And now, as an imperfect mother myself, I no longer hold her in contempt. She is forgiven and loved by me in all of her imperfection. But even after so much healing, my friendships with women can still be complicated. *I* can be complicated. But there is hope, and we are powerful enough to change. We do not have to be stuck in cycles that bring destruction to our relational connectedness, and that is good news! No matter what is at the root of your relational dysfunction, it does not have to stay that way.

So, what about you? Where do you find yourself? What does this bring up for you? God simply hasn't given up on you and me, and we don't have to be women with excuses—which can be annoying at times. "God, just let me play the victim for a hot second, okay? No? All right." He is always knocking on the door of our hearts, ready to recover and restore to us a new normal. We can avoid the drama we create and often attract while establishing peace, boundaries, and safety to our relationships.

This is where you come in. You're complex too, and we don't need the Enneagram to tell us this is true. Be honest with yourself for a second. Why is that? Because you are, we are, intricately made human beings formed in the image of an almighty God and then placed into a fallen world, where we walk out an imperfect journey with other intricate, complex people. That alone brings up a bag of issues for each of us that can either push us out of relationships or cause us to surrender our will and become more like Christ in them. Oh, but then just mix in the free will of others, your free will, and a good dose of broken trust on both ends, and just like that, you have a mess on your hands! And when it comes to friendships of the female kind, well, have you ever said, "I'm friends with guys. Women are just so, well, complicated"? Don't lie, we've all said it.

I've heard the saying "The glory of God is man fully alive." When we are wide awake to who we are made to be, even in our imperfection, we reflect the glory of God to humankind. We are created in His image after all; therefore, our identity is actually found in Him—not in our broken past or our chaotic present moment but all lovingly wrapped up in Him.

Let's take a moment to reflect before we move on.

REFLECTION POINTS

- What aspects of your personality and unique makeup as a created being in the image of God do you love? These are the beautiful things you also bring to the table in friendship! And, to be clear, you are completely and totally loved, whether you love everything about yourself or not. You'll get there!

- What areas of your life have you seen as weaknesses? How can God strengthen you in these areas? Where do you have brokenness in the way that you see yourself? Consider taking a moment to surrender that to God and ask Him to show you the truth.

- Where does brokenness in relationships with women come into play for you? Maybe you had an amazing relationship with your mother or sister(s), and other women seem to fall short. Maybe there has been perpetual brokenness in your relationships with women since you were born, and you're not sure where to enter into authentic friendship or how to heal. Consider vulnerably sharing that with someone and praying together that a path to healing would be made clear.

> I will praise you
> because I have been remarkably and wondrously made.
> Your works are wondrous,
> and I know this very well. (Ps. 139:14 CSB)

Women Helping Women, Not Women Hurting Women

The truth is, we need each other. And to fulfill our purpose together, without jealousy, comparison, envy, gossip, and unforgiveness, we're going to have to take responsibility for our lives and stop blaming the past for why we can't move forward and have a better future. It's a powerful choice to get back up and love someone again after experiencing a history of relational brokenness.

The ability for us to choose to keep loving others, no matter the relational pain we've been through, pushes us out of a victim mindset, reminding us of the authority we have to change, move forward, heal, and push through. Will we get hurt again? Absolutely. Is the pain worth it? Absolutely. I would take the pain of connection with other imperfect humans any day over the pain of isolation. In the words of Michael Scott on *The Office*, "No question about it, I'm ready to get hurt again." So, how does this connect to women helping women?

I'm a vivid dreamer and have been since I can remember. At times, my dreams are affected by too much ridiculously good New York pizza, but most of the time, they are God speaking to me at night, even as I rest. Dreams are found all throughout the Bible, Old and New Testament, and if you don't believe me, go and study it for yourself. I've noticed that I tend to have three types of dreams: God dreams, flesh dreams (processing the day and such), and demonic dreams. God dreams can warn, exhort, encourage, foretell, and so much more—we cannot box God in! Flesh dreams, as I'm calling them here (again, not a scientist and don't claim to be), are just a way the brain processes and sorts through what happened throughout our day. Often, a show we watched, a book we read, or conversations we had, internally or with others, can make their way into our dreams. Then there are demonic dreams that come to steal, kill, and destroy our peace. I have learned to be grateful for these dreams because they show me how to pray when the enemy reveals his hand.

Before I wrote this book, I had a dream. I hadn't been thinking about the writing process whatsoever before the dream, but God was revealing something to me, and in turn to you.

In the dream, I was sitting at a doctor's appointment. When I looked down, I realized I was in a wheelchair. I remember being confused because, in the dream, I knew I could walk and had no need of a wheelchair. As I looked up, a female doctor, maybe twenty years my senior, was there giving me the bad news that I would need to be in the wheelchair for the rest of my life. I looked with a fierce boldness at this "expert" in my health and well-being and spoke the truth clearly to her: "I do *not* need to be in this wheelchair. Look how strong I am!" I proceeded to get up, push the wheelchair aside, and do squat jumps, leaping at least three feet off the ground. Even I was astounded by my strength, and I was confident that I was right. My strength offended her and made her furious. She told me to sit back down and continued saying things that were meant to bring shame. She told me I was wrong, that I wasn't strong, and that the diagnosis was that I needed to be in that wheelchair for the rest of my life. Her desire to control and manipulate me instead of nurture, love, and pour into me was apparent. She made it clear that she was the expert and I was not. The truth is, her words did not hurt me nor cause me to fear. I was confident in who I was, and I knew my strength.

As I pondered the meaning of this dream, I realized that we often talk about the pain from our fathers, brothers, boyfriends, husbands, male leaders, pastors, and male coworkers, but we often neglect to talk about and heal from the pain that our mothers, mentors, female pastors, leaders, girlfriends, daughters, and sisters can bring. It's a different kind of wounding and one that needs deep healing too.

Maybe there are women who have told you to sit down. Women who have used control and manipulation to tell you that you won't make it or that you would be nothing without them. It's possible that there have been women who have ignored you. Women who have overshared in inappropriate ways and made you feel uncomfortable when you were too young or immature to carry their words. Maybe certain women have told you that your voice and your life are insignificant—usually because those women needed to feel more significant than you or wanted you to think that you can't *be* or *do* anything meaningful without them. Maybe some women have enticed you to be in their "club" and then made it impossible to belong. What about women who have sucked the life out of you, all in the name of friendship, but gave nothing in return? Oh, and we've all had that one "friend" who only shows up when she needs you for your connections or what you can give. (Thank you. I feel so loved.) It's possible you've had female teachers who told you that you'd always be average and never excel in this, that, or the other thing. Women who didn't protect you, advocate for you, or have your back when you needed it. Some of you have had mothers who left you, and the hole in your heart from the abandonment feels beyond repair. Maybe there are women who have shamed you and sat you down when you needed healing, restoration, and grace. And it hurts. It hurts more than you ever let on because you are "strong on your own," but deep down there is an aching for more. You are aching for genuine connection of the sisterhood kind, even if it's messy and imperfect (because it will be). But something in you knows it's biblical, knows it's God ordained, knows that we are designed to be women who lift up other women. You and I both know that deep down we need each other.

I hate to say it, but I have been blacklisted, ignored, cast aside, laughed at, slandered, not taken seriously, sat down, talked down to, and talked about all by women I've trusted, let in, or looked up to, and I'd guess you have too. But does that mean we stop living? Stop connecting? Stop healing? No. If we want to become women genuinely helping women, we need to be willing to do the good work of healing and restoration on our own end. Otherwise, if we're not careful, we will become what we despise—women hurting women—and we'll do to others exactly what was done to wound us.

We need to find our strength again, remember who we are, and champion each other's causes as women. You are not my competition. I have no fear of you and your powerful squat jumps. I don't need to put you in your place. You are my sister, my daughter, my mother, my friend.

Women, it's time for us to heal, restore, and uncomplicate that which has been stolen or lost when it comes to female relationships. We need to heal from the wounds our mothers, mentors, and sisters gave us. We need to let Jesus take the knives out of our backs that people we once trusted placed there. We need to rise up and show our daughters a new way.

We all have scars from relational brokenness. Just remember that your scars tell a story. They are the strongest part of your skin. Wounds need attention and care to irradicate infection so that healing can run its course, but scars tell a story of healing. If you have wounds, let them be healed. If you have scars, maybe it's time to awaken to the truth that you are being called to come alongside another sister, share your story, and show her how to heal, letting her know that she doesn't have to be on the outside looking in anymore.

Yes, it can be complicated, because we are complex, intricate human beings with a past, but we also have an unwritten future and an opportunity within this present moment to begin to forge new pathways. We are the common denominator in every relationship we are in, and the good news is—we can change.

REFLECTION POINTS

- How has your past pain with other women stopped you from helping and championing women today? Ask Father God what healing He has for you in this area of your life. Consider taking some time to sit before Him and to listen and receive that healing.
- What did the dream about the woman putting me in the wheelchair bring up for you? Does it make you feel

like doing squat jumps, or does it ring too true for your season right now?

- What scars do you have that tell a story of healing? Share that with someone. And what potential wounds do you have that now need to be healed? Initiate an action plan to walk in healing in this area of your life, and share it with someone who will genuinely check in on you and see how it's going.

> Search me, O God, and know my heart!
> Try me and know my thoughts!
> And see if there be any grievous way in me,
> and lead me in the way everlasting! (Ps. 139:23–24 ESV)

Here is a prayer for you to pray:

Lord, I am uniquely complex and wonderfully made in Your eyes—even the parts of me and my life that I try to avoid, feel ashamed of, or cover up. It's my desire to walk in authentic connection with You and with other women. If there are barriers to doing this in any way, I surrender them to You and ask You to reveal to me any path I am walking on that is causing pain or prolonging it. Show me the way of healing. I give this journey to You, Lord. Lead, direct, nurture, and deliver me. I am wholly and completely Yours.

chapter 3

NAVIGATING BETRAYAL

A true friend stabs you in the front, not in the back.

Oscar Wilde

"Andi"—*pregnant pause*—"that was a major betrayal of you and Paul." Those words hit deep.

I had been in EMT mode, taking care of everyone else at the scene of the figurative crash site, until my therapist said those words: *a major betrayal.* They cut past my semihardened flesh and nicked a part of my heart that I had unconsciously been protecting by "doing the right things" to get through, be okay, and care for everyone else who had been touched by the ripple effect of this particular betrayal. My husband and I were at ground zero, trying to pick up the pieces and put together a game plan to clear away the rubble, heal, and rebuild. Trust had been broken, and I realized as we walked through this situation together that survival mode *can be* helpful to function, but it's not a sustainable way to live. The truth is, I knew that the grief and pain were being held at bay right there under the surface; the dam just hadn't burst yet. I know that when I begin to feel numb, I'm going to get hit with a surge of grief and anger at some stage—possibly rage and waves of uncontained, unpredictable emotions—I just don't know when, where, or how it will all come out. And listen, if you're near me when it does, brace yourself. But as my therapist said those words, it felt like a small crack in the dam increased. I became more aware of the pain of betrayal. I had felt like that's what it was—*betrayal*—but hadn't really said it as bluntly and truthfully as those stark words: *a major betrayal.*

I have an aversion to rejection and betrayal, and I'd go so far as to say you do too. I'm pretty sure that my prayer right after this particular session with my therapist sounded something like, "But, Lord, I don't want to walk through the grief and pain and the potential mess of rebuilding a relationship after a betrayal. I mean, *I do,* but also I don't." Unfortunately, this was not my first rodeo with betrayal, so I knew the road ahead of me was long and unmapped because imperfect humans with free will were involved, as always.

Navigating the waters of betrayal is tantamount to navigating the waters of a ferocious storm. Even though you've probably done it before, the new storm brings new waves and uncharted territory to navigate because the sea is wild and untamed. Franklin D. Roosevelt said, "A smooth sea never made a skilled sailor."[1] But what if I don't want to be a sailor? What if I don't want the storm? I mean, the thing that sucks about a storm is that you can't control its course and you didn't ask for it to come; it just does. You have to go into a certain mode to survive, but then after the storm passes and you make it out alive, you have to process the trauma of sailing those seas when you didn't ask to sail them—when it wasn't in the plan. But you can come out stronger *if* you choose to.

So, let's navigate betrayal together, shall we? And not just from the perspective of the one being betrayed, but also from the view of the betrayer. First, we all must start with the state of our own heart.

King David or Judas?

Now, before we all start making a list of the Judases in our lives, let's remember that we have possibly been (and probably are) a Judas to someone else. (Judas was one of the twelve disciples, and he ultimately betrayed Jesus unto His death after three years of walking in close fellowship with Him.) It is highly plausible that we were invited into someone else's life and became the root cause of their pain. That is a hard truth to face, especially because we can't control the outcome of what happens to that relationship when pain and the free will of two people are at play. We can't force them to forgive us or invite us back in. Relational mess simply reinforces the fact that we are human and deeply in need of Jesus and His saving grace on a daily basis. Let's all just remember when we point the finger at someone else, we always have three fingers pointing back at our own heart.

I'm going to start with the premise that *an unchecked heart is a dangerous heart.* Yours and theirs. The betrayed and betrayer— whichever side of the fence you find yourself on.

To forgive a betrayer in your life, you have to have a contrite, tender, repentant heart first. You have to take care of your side of the fence, or the "log in your eye," if you will, before you can remove the speck in someone else's eye. If you have left your heart unchecked for too long, it's possible that bitterness, judgment, pride, and entitlement are lingering somewhere in there. It's possible you've gotten to a place where you believe that when you are hurt or betrayed by someone, you are justified in punishing them and making them pay for their sin toward you. Pride blinds us to our own sin.

Psalm 51 is paramount in understanding *contrition*, which is simply operating from a space of having a tender, repentant heart before God for your sin. In a moment, we'll see that Psalm 51 is King David's response to God after being called out for his sin and ultimate betrayal of a fellow warrior, neighbor, and friend.

In 2 Samuel 11, David had committed the egregious acts of adultery and murder. He had hoped he could cover up his sin of adultery with Bathsheba by putting Uriah, the husband of Bathsheba, on the front line of a losing battle where David knew Uriah would die. Bathsheba was now pregnant with David's child from the affair, and she had not slept with her husband in the window of time when she would have conceived. Uriah would've known she was an adulterer, and it probably would have brought her to an untimely death by stoning, according to the Law. David's sin created a ripple effect that was unstoppable. Left unchecked, sin makes a bigger and bigger mess until it comes out.

I would assume that we all know from experience (unless I live in a bubble) that sin always comes to light. It's like a festering pimple in plain sight on your nose that you can't make disappear no matter how many magical creams you try—it will have its day of eruption, and it will be seen.

Jesus said, "Be on your guard against the yeast of the Pharisees, which is hypocrisy. There is nothing concealed that will not be disclosed, or hidden that will not be made known. What you have said in the dark will be heard in the daylight, and what you have whispered in the ear in the inner rooms will be proclaimed from the roofs" (Luke 12:1–3). Jesus is constantly addressing our heart issues throughout each Gospel if we have eyes to see, ears to hear, and a heart to understand. The fruit of what's going on inside of us, the things we've spoken about and done in the darkness, will have their day in the light.

When the prophet Nathan confronted David in his sin, David wept and cried out to God for mercy. "Have mercy on me, O God, according to your unfailing love; according to your great compassion blot out my transgressions. Wash away all my iniquity and cleanse me from my sin" (Ps. 51:1–2). He asks God to create in him a pure heart, to restore the joy of God's salvation in his life (vv. 10 and 12). When King David was confronted with the tragedy and mess of his sin, it brought him to his knees in repentance. His heart was deeply broken for all the pain he had caused. He understood that it didn't matter how many sacrifices he made on the altar at the temple in front of God and man; no PR plan could salvage this. It was a contrite, penitent heart the Lord desired. And it was what would change David's life, no matter how big a mess he had made.

> You do not delight in sacrifice, or I would bring it;
>   you do not take pleasure in burnt offerings.
> My sacrifice, O God, is a broken spirit;
>   a broken and contrite heart
>   you, God, will not despise. (Ps. 51:16–17)

This radical ownership of his own life, this gut-wrenching honesty of his need for God's mercy, caused David to be known as a man after God's own heart. David was a betrayer of others' trust. He was a mess and so was his life. He was a sinner in need of grace. The more I pivot and look at Judas, the more I realize he was a mess too, but he chose to take the reins of his own life instead of laying them down in front of Jesus and asking for forgiveness.

Judas started off on the right foot, or so it seems. He was called as one of the twelve original disciples to follow Jesus and made the radical commitment to leave his life and follow the Rabbi. And we can't say if it was disingenuous or not because we don't know Judas's original heart motive for following Jesus. He was given so much opportunity: to heal the sick, to raise the dead, and to cast out demons. He witnessed some of the greatest miracles ever seen and was taught firsthand the message of the kingdom of heaven straight from the lips of the Messiah. He had the perfect discipleship environment, yet he made a choice to betray the One who brought him closer than a brother. Even Jesus cannot control the matters of the human heart. Jesus sows the seed; we steward the soil of our hearts. Maybe this rings true for some of you when it comes to relationships of the female kind with those you allowed so close but then questioned whether it was too close. To keep it simple, remember this: we have to keep our own hearts in check and realize we are powerless to do that for anyone else.

Years ago, I walked through betrayal in a friendship with someone I had let very close to me. Someone who "dined at my table," if you will, and who had the power to hurt me because I gave that power to them. When a storm came in that relationship and dramatically shifted the trajectory of its original destination, I began to grieve, wondering why I ever let them so close. I felt the Holy Spirit say to me, "Andi, even my Son, Jesus, had room for Judas at His table. Even Judas had a free will to repent . . ." *Psssh! Not what I want to hear, Holy Spirit.* Basically, this means I can't *really* trust anyone.

Actually, what it means is that I really can't *control* anyone. It also means none of us have faced our last betrayal, so we need to continually set a guard over our own hearts. As Proverbs 4:23 tells us, "Above all else, guard your heart, for *everything you do flows from it.*" And get good at navigating the waters of betrayal.

On reflection, I can't help but think that Judas had an opportunity for repentance and that Jesus brought him close enough for Judas to betray Him but also to be forgiven by Him. We can learn so much from both David and Judas. Both were betrayers, both were in need of love and forgiveness from God, both had the option to repent—but one chose life and one chose death.

Now, your blood may be boiling reading this, and you may be thinking, *Andi, all I wanted to do was write a list of my betrayers to understand how to navigate how they hurt* me. Yes, we will go there, but as with every single issue in life, *everything* we do flows from the heart. Therefore, the posture of our own heart is paramount when it comes to our ability to forgive, set boundaries, consider reconciliation (or not), and love even when we don't want to. This all starts with us, not with "them," because we cannot control "them" and their choices.

Also, the standard Jesus sets for those who have broken our trust, hurt us, and become possible enemies in our lives is ridiculously high. Luke 6:32–36 says,

> If you love those who love you, what credit is that to you? Even sinners love those who love them. And if you do good to those who are good to you, what credit is that to you? Even sinners do that. And if you lend to those from whom you expect repayment, what credit is that to you? Even sinners lend to sinners,

expecting to be repaid in full. *But love your enemies, do good to them, and lend to them without expecting to get anything back. Then your reward will be great, and you will be children of the Most High, because he is kind to the ungrateful and wicked. Be merciful, just as your Father is merciful.*

That is a hard scriptural pill to swallow, straight from the lips of Jesus. Love your enemies and do good to them? Are you kidding me? Give them mercy? Why should I? How about I pray that You, O God, will bring Your justice down on them like a hammer for hurting me? How about You give them what they deserve for being so selfish and hurting so many people? How about . . . yeah, this isn't healthy. We serve, follow, and give our lives to a God who doesn't give us what we deserve, but while our backs were turned on Him in our own sin and betrayal, He died for us. Rescued us. Forgave us. Reached out in love toward us.

It's up to me to forgive. No one can make me do it, and I may not *feel* like doing it, but it is an act of my free will. Forgiveness does not mean agreement with another's sin or behavior—quite the opposite. It is a sign of our tender heart toward God, even when someone owes us a debt that they will never be able to pay. "Be kind to one another, tenderhearted, forgiving one another, as God in Christ forgave you" (Eph. 4:32 ESV).

Dr. Henry Cloud and Dr. John Townsend say, "The Bible is clear about two principles: (1) We always need to forgive, but (2) we don't always achieve reconciliation. Forgiveness is something that we do in our hearts; we release someone from a debt that they owe us. We write off the person's debt, and she no longer owes us. We no longer condemn her. She is clean. Only one party is needed for forgiveness: me. The person who owes me a debt does not have to ask my forgiveness. It is a work of grace in my heart."[2]

Whether you are the betrayer or betrayed, traversing the waters of brokenness in relationships is something we all have to do. In doing that, as we steward our hearts, here is something my therapist said to me that I think we all need to understand:

> The enemy will take you further than you thought you would go, will keep you longer than you thought you would stay, and will charge you more than you thought you were willing to pay.

Set a guard over that heart of yours, friend. It is the most valuable asset (or liability) you have stewardship over. No one else can do it for you.

The selfishness and self-preservation of sin are destructive and painful to those in their wake—that's why the duplicitous nature of betrayal hurts so badly. You think you know someone and what their motives are only to find out they weren't who you thought they were, and their motives were different than you had perceived. Their unchecked heart-life erupts all over you. And when the fruit of sin reveals itself, it feels like the shock of a car crash—a sideswipe that you didn't see coming. You feel the pain in every cell of your body, and it causes you to recoil and curl up in the fetal position under the warm covers of your bed and hide from the world, vowing never to be touched again. It can take time to peel back the layers of that betrayal and reveal what's going on in your own heart. And if or when that friendship dies, you have to go through a cycle of grief—grief to move on or grief to have any chance of resurrected life within that friendship.

Grief Is *Not* Your Enemy

Once we identify the position of our own heart—contrite or hardened—and identify our place in the relationship(s) we are navigating—betrayer or betrayed—then we have to begin to grieve what was or what could've been so that we can move forward and not stay stuck in a cycle of unprocessed grief.

Have you ever just been done with people? Like the pain of healing from broken trust over and over again is just too much? I know I have. Life can be filled with grief and heartache, as well as a whole lot of beauty. The best of times and the worst of times all in one day (thank you, Dickens). I've learned the hard way that if we don't grieve properly, we become cynical and grief becomes our enemy.

The broken, distrustful version of myself would say that pastoring a church feels like you're being set up for relational failure and constant rejection. I know this may sound ridiculous or overly dramatic, but this is the space where I have grieved and hurt more in my life than I ever thought I would. It's also the space where I've experienced more hope, joy, love, genuine community, and promises fulfilled than anywhere else. When we planted Liberty Church in New York City in 2010, I had such high idealistic hopes of building a thriving community with lifelong friendships. Of having meals at my house, breaking bread together, studying the Word, praying for one another, and seeing signs, wonders, and miracles take place as we all took care of each other's needs. Yes, Acts 2:42–47 painted this very vision I could see in my mind's eye.

It's beautiful, right? And I must say, that is how I began building the church. But about ten years in, with earth-shattering lows and ridiculously climactic highs accompanied by unattainable expectations placed on my shoulders by myself and others, I started to notice that I was "building" the church in the exact opposite spirit. I became full of fear—fear of what people thought of my leadership, fear of failure, fear of more rejection, fear of people coming, promising the world, and then leaving. Anytime someone wanted to have coffee with me or needed to talk, I would flinch and have a minor panic attack. I began building my life in a way in which I was protecting myself from more pain because *everyone* (exaggeration for dramatic effect) I have sincerely loved has either left me or cut me so deeply. I'm still bleeding, so self-preservation it is. (That's in the Bible, right? Nope.)

I remember waking up one morning while on a trip in London, crippled with heaviness, sadness, and fear. I had allowed myself to operate in negative thought patterns and detrimental heart meditations about my relationships (specifically the broken ones and those with naysayers) for so long that heaviness and hopelessness had set in. I told myself for the millionth time that I was actually done with people.

I sent a text message to one of my mentors and mothers in the faith, Maria Durso, whom I affectionately call Mama Maria.

Good morning. Can I ask you to pray for me? I am having a low day and just don't want to pastor or lead anymore. It hits me hard sometimes.

She *immediately* responded.

I'm in Chicago, weeping. I've been crying since 5 a.m. I will pray right now. "Don't get tired of doing good ... at just the right time (today's just not that time, lol), we will reap a blessing IF WE DON'T GIVE UP" (Gal. 6:9). Let Him carry you today; allow Him to feed you today!!!

She proceeded to call me right after she sent the above text, and when I said hello, she launched into prayer over me, weeping, encouraging, prophesying, and speaking life. She had the words I needed at just that moment to continue.

As I got off the phone, the Holy Spirit's still, small voice whispered, *Andi, grief is not your enemy.*

My goodness. I had been avoiding grief like the plague—or, more accurately, I had been stuck in its cycle. I had stayed immersed in the first four stages of grief, in no particular order, but never seemed to get to stage 5, which actually changes the game.

Elisabeth Kübler-Ross and David Kessler list the five stages of grief as

- denial
- anger
- bargaining
- depression
- acceptance[3]

After consistently being in shock due to relational brokenness (pastoring is so fun), I realized I was also in a constant state of denial because my life didn't look the way I thought it would. Church, community, and friendship were panning out in a way I couldn't control. It made me angry because, deep down, a sadness lurked where my idealistic expectations of myself and others were consistently being crushed. So, anger came out as my self-protective mechanism. I bargained with the Lord for another way, another calling, away from humanity, on a big block of land in nature, far, far away from people. And I have to say, the weight of denial, anger, and bargaining with

God turned into depression and discouragement that wouldn't go away. I refused to accept my reality—that life is hard, and equally beautiful, but hard nonetheless—and move forward. C. S. Lewis said,

> No one ever told me that grief felt so like fear. I am not afraid, but the sensation is like being afraid. The same fluttering in the stomach, the same restlessness, the yawning. I keep on swallowing.
>
> At other times it feels like being mildly drunk, or concussed. There is a sort of invisible blanket between the world and me. I find it hard to take in what anyone says. Or perhaps, hard to want to take it in. It is so uninteresting. Yet I want the others to be about me. I dread the moments when the house is empty. If only they would talk to one another and not to me.[4]

Grief can be disorienting, erratic, and uncontrollable. And it doesn't just come with the death of a loved one; it can also come through divorce, illness, dismissal from work, a move, a new line of work, a global pandemic (i.e., 2020), a change in responsibilities at work, the birth of a child, the loss of independence, or a child leaving home (the thought already makes me cry). Basically, any major or even minor life transitions and, of course, betrayal or broken trust of any kind. Grief often makes us feel like we're caught in the fog of war, unaware of which direction our enemy is coming from. But when we walk in radical acceptance of our actual reality, instead of fantasizing about another season or life, and refuse to deny its pain, trouble, mess, or heartache, the fog of war begins to dissipate, and we know which fronts we need to fight on. We begin to see clearly again, with a renewed hope to find meaning right where we are.

I am not an expert on grief, but I have plenty of experience walking through it, and I'm sure you do too. I highly recommend researching different books that can help you walk through its stages in a healthy way.

So, after checking the posture of our own hearts, choosing to forgive as many times as it takes, and walking through the stages of grief, or at least recognizing where we are in its cycle, it's time to put on love—yes, again—as we navigate betrayal together.

Love, Love, and More Love

After talking to my therapist, who opened my eyes to help me see that I had faced a "major betrayal," I looked up and read 1 Corinthians 13:4–8, which is on the wall of my bedroom, positioned at the foot of the bed so my husband and I can wake up to its reminder every morning:

> Love is patient, love is kind. It does not envy, it does not boast, it is not proud. It does not dishonor others, it is not self-seeking, it is not easily angered, it keeps no record of wrongs. Love does not delight in evil but rejoices with the truth. It always protects, always trusts, always hopes, always perseveres. Love never fails.

To read these words is one thing, but to live them, apply them, and let them come alive in us, well, it's Christlike and it's hard. To live a "Father, forgive them for they know not what they do, and some of them know exactly what they do, but they do it anyway" sort of life is almost impossible. Why? Because it cannot be done without the love of Christ living, healing, and thriving within us first. We need to let Him love us like this so that we can give away love like this. So, let's take a moment to reflect on these words, line by line, in our own lives and consider how we can practically apply them.

REFLECTION POINTS

As you read through each of the aspects of love below, take some time to consider where you need to receive God's love and where you need to give it. I encourage you to write these as bullet points in a journal or in a note in your phone. Then underneath each one, write how you can give or receive each aspect of love in a practical way. For example, consider the first line. Where do you need God's love to be patient with you? Then, to whom do you need to apply this and administer large amounts of incredibly patient love, even if said person is testing every ounce of your patience? Reflect, write it down, and if need be, pray it through. Remember, when we receive first from our good and deeply loving God, we have so much more to give. Even Christ, being both God and man, operated within human limits. He stepped away from His disciples and the crowds to connect with, commune with, and receive from His Father—and we, as followers of Jesus, are empowered to do likewise.

- Love is patient.
- Love is kind.
- Love does not envy.
- Love does not boast.
- Love is not proud.
- Love does not dishonor others.
- Love is not self-seeking.
- Love is not easily angered.
- Love keeps no record of wrongs.
- Love does not delight in evil but rejoices with the truth.

- Love always protects.
- Love always trusts.
- Love always hopes.
- Love always perseveres.
- Love never fails.

A Quick Word on Boundaries

In essence, a boundary is a definitive line that defines who owns, controls, and is responsible for something. Fences on property lines exist for a reason: to let each owner know what they need to take care of on the plot of land they own but also not to cross into territory where they have no ownership or jurisdiction. As you navigate betrayal in friendship, you have to get clear on what you own and what the other person owns. I mean, to make this relevant right now, ask yourself if, in the last thirty days, you have tried to fix something for someone that wasn't (emotionally or even practically) yours to fix. Maybe you've tried to clean up their mess for them or carry a burden that wasn't yours to carry. Have you taken responsibility for someone's moods, actions, or words when it was actually out of your hands to do so? Have you said yes to something or someone when you meant or wanted to say no? How does it feel? How did it work out for you? No sarcasm intended; genuinely, how did it go?

Listen, just because you have chosen to set a guard over your heart, forgive, and lean in to love for someone in spite of a betrayal doesn't mean that they are necessarily going to be your friend again. What it means is that after you have done all of the above before the Lord, you have to put appropriate boundaries in place to move forward in a healthy, safe manner.

What are you willing and unwilling to do in the relationship? Or is there a necessary ending in sight for this relationship because it is no longer safe or healthy?

When you start to set boundaries with someone, be prepared for what will come. It may be difficult to watch as the mess they are in grows or gets worse. Maybe it'll be hard to watch as they choose not to take ownership of their side of things, which may cause you to feel the urge to try to jump back in, smooth things over, or help them see the light. Don't do it; you're not really helping. Let the consequences of their decisions take their course. Your boundaries won't just help you to walk in clarity, health, and healing; they will help all parties involved, even if the experience is grueling. Step out of codependency and into personal responsibility.

As much as the weight of betrayal feels like something you'll carry forever, setting healthy boundaries will change the game for you and for them. And when you sense yourself starting to carry the burden for someone else's choices, you may simply practice saying out loud this line that we use in prayer ministry as we walk people through a forgiveness prayer: "Their issues (whoever they are) are not my issues. They are not for me to fix and they are not for me to carry." Remember, you cannot manipulate someone else's free will or force them to clean up their act; you can only clean up and take care of your side of the fence.

My husband preached on boundaries to our community of believers, and in short, here are his reasons why boundaries matter:

1. *Boundaries are about valuing ourselves* and *others.*
   When we practice healthy boundaries, we are empowered to build relationships grounded in love.

2. *Boundaries inform us.* If someone crosses one of my boundaries, the world doesn't fall apart, but it's as though a warning light appears on my dash. It's information.

3. *Boundaries protect us.* We are each called to guard our hearts. So, that includes our values, thoughts, feelings, passions, sins, weaknesses, history, and strengths.[5]

Often, we don't set boundaries because we fear conflict or the loss of a relationship. Neither of those is a good enough reason to avoid setting boundaries in our lives. The truth is, the person may leave; they may say harsh, untrue, or cruel things; they may slander you and sling guilt your way; but when you set boundaries, you become aware of what is theirs and what is yours. You are able to walk powerfully, even through painful seasons.

Betrayal doesn't have to destroy you or take you out. It hurts like crazy, but, friend, you will get through this and come out stronger and, dare I say, a better friend.

Recap: How Do We Navigate the Waters of Betrayal?

I haven't faced my last betrayal yet, and neither have you. Betrayal is a part of the human experience. To recap and reflect before we move on, remember to

- *Check your heart posture.* Look inside your own heart first—repent of your own sin.
- *Choose to forgive over and over if needed.* Remember, it's an act of your free will. You probably won't feel like it.

- *Grieve fully and completely.* Figure out where you are in the stages of grief and commit to walking through each one of them.

- *Choose love, even if strong boundaries need to be in place, because love simply never fails.* Receive love and then choose to give it away. We love because He first loved us.

- *Set boundaries all day, every day.* Someone else's issues are not your issues. They are not for you to fix; they are not for you to carry.

chapter 4

THE TRUTH ABOUT
SELF-PRESERVATION

Self-preservation is willfully choosing the pain of isolation over the potential of messy godly connection.

Andi Andrew

Over coffee one day, a friend reminded me of something I said to our church when we were just beginning as a community of believers here in New York: "We're all scaling the mountain of our own brokenness to step into our inheritance. You can either charge the mountain with us or circle the bottom and watch."

Honestly, I needed that advice for myself in that moment.

Why do we circle the bottom of our mountains instead of scaling them? Is it fear? Almost always, yes. But maybe, just maybe, part of the root of that fear is self-preservation. I mean, if we scale that mountain, we could get hurt or face things that might scare us—confront us, even—and cause us to have to rise up, fight, and change. So, we keep it safe, circling the mountain because we *know* how to do that. Base camp is a familiar space from which we look up at the dream while fantasizing about what it would be like to step into it and live it.

Unfortunately, I have a PhD in self-preservation. And in our humanity, unsubmitted to Christ, we all do. Why do you think Adam and Eve covered themselves up after they sinned in the garden? To self-preserve and cover the shame of their choices that ultimately led to sin. It was never God's intention that we live on our own, separated from Him, covering ourselves while toiling to survive without help from or connection to Him and others. He wants to walk with us in the "cool of the garden" of our lives and be in constant communion. If we're not self-aware, regularly in the Word of God, and being led by the Holy Spirit daily, we will naturally self-preserve.

Don't believe me? Let me tell you a little story about what should've been a perfect day—do those even exist? Remember, I'm a grown woman but don't always act like one. I can be a self-preserving three-year-old who doesn't know how to function, and it's ugly.

The truth is, in the scariest part of me, the place where my fears lurk and linger, I'm convinced I'm unlovable *unless* I present myself as perfect and put together to you—and at times, even to my husband and children.

Christmas Day of 2019 was absolute perfection—well, the morning was, up until about ten o'clock. Everything I had seamlessly planned was going according to schedule. The kids ran up the stairs with genuine joy to "It's Beginning to Look a Lot Like Christmas." Yes, I staged it for my own benefit *and* social media—shallow, I know. And yes, it was the Bing Crosby version, of course. The children had hung their stockings with care the night before but opened them with a lot less care. While the kids ripped open their small stocking gifts, the cinnamon rolls were rising to perfection in the oven. Even the keto ones, prepared the night before, were ready to be devoured—only by me of course, because I'm the only one who likes them. The bacon was cooked to impeccable crispiness—not too crispy, but definitely not too soft. We sat around a beautifully set table with Paul's nan's hand-painted china, fresh-brewed French press coffee, berries, Greek yogurt, and mascarpone. We prayed and thanked God for His Son, the reason why we celebrate all day (hello, Andi, please don't forget this), and devoured the food.

As we all started to clean up (because I have four children who have two hands each, and I don't care that it's Christmas Day, you will pull your weight), I decided to read the directions for the slow-cooker lamb I was making for dinner. To my dismay, I had lost an hour by not getting it in on time. An *hour*, folks. For me, this started a small internal spiral but one that I could cover up with a smile and efficiency in the kitchen. I whipped out the lamb, prepped it, and threw it in the slow cooker in ten minutes flat. I texted everyone who was coming for dinner and let them know it was going to be an hour later than I had planned. Crisis #1 averted.

We sat around the tree, fresh coffee in hand, and took turns opening our presents, one by one, stretching out the time. We listened to Frank Sinatra's Christmas playlist and basked in the glory of our eleven-foot-tall, six-foot-wide, gorgeous, and, yes, perfectly (in my mind) decorated, "could be dropped in a mall" tree. We read the last pages of Ann Voskamp's Advent book, shared our gratitude for Jesus—our greatest gift—and prayed with thanksgiving. It was literally perfect. And then it happened.

A picture frame on the coffee table tipped over, in turn knocking my cup of hot black coffee to the floor, right on my rug. My rug with no stains. My rug that, if I like you, I'll let you wear shoes on (maybe). I started to cry. My kids—yes, all four of them—ran to get something to clean it up with. They knew. *Keep Mom calm. Keep things in order.* They did all they could to help, and we got it taken care of. Crisis #2 averted.

The world came back into order for a while. The kids played with their new things, and we all rested, showered, and got ready for a few friends to join us in the evening for dinner. I played the *Nutcracker* movie on my laptop while I prepped dinner and set the table. All was calm, all was bright. Paul came up to help me, and then Crisis #3 began. He accidentally—key word here, *accidentally*—knocked over a glass of water (not wine, grape juice, or anything that stains) on my flawlessly set table, and somehow that was it. Look, I had planned everything out months before, from presents to food to when we would do each thing. I had timed everything out (probably should've put up a run sheet in the kitchen to keep everyone on track), and now our guests were arriving in fifteen minutes and we had to strip the whole table, throw the tablecloth in the dryer, and turn this thing around before they all walked in. And the cheese platters weren't ready! I mean, it was over.

I was furious.

Furious.

Not sad, disappointed, or slightly empathetic to my husband's simple mistake—but *furious.*

And Paul felt it. I made him the fool. And my children saw it. They tried to calm the storm. In that moment, I could see into the future. I saw myself paying their therapy bills for the trauma I was causing in this very moment. This was not the

Christmas I had planned. Not for them. And not for our guests, who were about to arrive. I didn't have time to cover up my mess. Everyone saw it in all its glory. These are the spirals I fear. The ones I try to avoid. This is what I'm most afraid of. *You* seeing my incompetence as a mother, as a homemaker, as a wife, as a human. With no time to cover it up, self-preserve, smile, or wave. This is why we can't get too close, why we can't be friends . . . because you might peek behind the curtain and see this hot mess.

All of a sudden, my brain couldn't process normal life. I forgot how to put the cheese platter together. Then I punctured my finger on the plastic of the quince paste container, and as I'm bleeding everywhere (not on the cheese; we can't have that), the doorbell rings. Yes, now is the perfect time to arrive—when everything is falling apart. Welcome to our home, *early* guest. Please, never show up at my home early. Our poor guest was walking into this moment. *This* moment. (Insert visual of Andi shaking her fist at the sky, running her other hand, the one that's bleeding, under cold water in the sink, while sobbing uncontrollably and breathing out a panicked, "Why, God, why?") With one spill, *my* order and peace had turned into mess and chaos. My children were wide-eyed with panic, wondering how to restore peace, but the truth is, no one could.

My table was unset, my brain in a jumble, and my (controlled) beauty disturbed—all by an honest mistake. I couldn't breathe properly. I walked out onto our back deck, crying like a child and swearing like a sailor, all while crying out to God to help me. To meet me in this mess. I mean, where is *my* perfect Christmas now?

"God, why am I such a Martha? Why can't I just be like Mary? I don't want my kids to scramble to cover up for me

73

or my husband to be a fall guy who is treated like a fool. This is why I can't have friends. Please! Help me!"

Well, after I let the love of God in, cried my eyes out, forgave my husband for his honest mistake, and forgave myself for being an angry, vengeful control freak, I went back into the public square of my household, shoulders back, red eyes holding back tears, blotchy cheeks facing upward, and asked for the forgiveness of my guests for my extremely human moment on Jesus's birthday. All was forgiven, hugs were shared all around, cookies were decorated, lamb was eaten, and a rousing game of Apples to Apples was played by all. Laughter ensued, connection was made, and grace was given. Jesus is still and always will be the greatest gift, and it's simply accentuated when I'm a mess. When *we* are a mess. Hiding doesn't help; it just perpetuates shame. Grace, forgiveness, and love heal and bring us out into the light with others who love us in all our imperfection.

Going Back to Move Forward

As I mentioned earlier, there was a lot of *felt* underlying chaos in my household growing up. I believe it's one of the reasons I love planning and order—it makes me feel safe. My parents truly did their best, but their marriage was on the rocks for a large part of my childhood. (They walk in miracle restoration now, but that was not our family's foundation.) I felt very alone as a child, full of unexpressed, pent-up, deep emotions. I naturally leaned toward being a performer and a controller. I made people laugh, I was good enough at sports, and, as a cheerleader, I could rally a crowd with passion to do just about anything. I sang and danced, won speech contests, and entered into every talent show with my friends. I baked multiple times a week and could put a smile on your face with sugar, which made me feel valued. I felt loved when I gave to others and it pleased them. I loved it when things were peaceful, or at least had the illusion of peace. But when the cracks started to appear and tranquility left the room, I didn't know what to do except withdraw and self-preserve. I would run to my room—my safe space because it was one place in my life that was in military order. It was always clean and organized. It was my place of peace. And it still is to this day.

Even today, I recognize that, under stress, these tendencies can still pop up for me. They've become rumble strips, warning me that I'm veering off the road of life into unhelpful places—for me and my loved ones. Deep down, I still sometimes have a desire to control everything, create peaceful environments (untouchable by humans—which isn't true peace), and make sure that everyone feels loved and seen, including myself. I also know that if I don't have a strategy in place, one small thing, like spilled coffee or water, can cause my personal universe to fly into chaos, making me feel like an utter failure when the truth is, all I need to do is take a moment, breathe, let myself be loved, and walk in grace.

God knows our every move before we make it. He knows our every word before we say it and each thought before we think it. He has promised that He will never leave us nor forsake us, even when we try to run away and control things on our own. This is such good news. Through God's tenderness and persistence, He proves to us that He's not going anywhere, gently drawing us out of our caves of self-preservation. As we choose to step into this truth, we intentionally and willfully push back on our human tendencies to hide from others and even our tendency to hide from God. Before we move on, let's take a moment to pause and reflect together.

REFLECTION POINTS

- What is your greatest fear in relationships? What is your inner critic screaming out in an attempt to keep others at bay, to control others, or to pull others close to try to "fix it" (whatever "it" is for you), even though no human can fix it—only Jesus can?

- What sort of circumstances or relational interactions cause you to self-preserve and hide from connecting with others?

- What strategy can you put into place that can help you when you begin to spiral or desire to isolate? "Spiraling," as I'm calling it here, can come out of the blue as a trauma response, where the emotional part of the brain overrides the logical part instead of the two working together. (Read *The Body Keeps the Score* by Bessel van der Kolk, MD.) Simply stopping, taking deep breaths, or even taking just five minutes alone to calm down can help. We have to allow ourselves to walk in grace and receive love. Then make amends where needed and move forward.

- Write out or read Psalm 139:1–7. Hide these words in your heart. Meditate on them, and give yourself some space to understand how great the Father's love is for you in all your self-preserving imperfection.

> You have searched me, LORD,
>   and you know me.
> You know when I sit and when I rise;
>   you perceive my thoughts from afar.
> You discern my going out and my lying down;
>   you are familiar with all my ways.

Before a word is on my tongue
   you, LORD, know it completely.
You hem me in behind and before,
   and you lay your hand upon me.
Such knowledge is too wonderful for me,
   too lofty for me to attain.
Where can I go from your Spirit?
Where can I flee from your presence?

The Slippery Slope of Self-Preservation—How Did I Get Here?

A two-book deal?! Speaking engagements all around the world?! Launching a sold-out women's conference?! Yes, yes, and yes!

All sounds good on paper, right? Yes. Except when all these things started to take off in my life, Paul and I were walking through a difficult time in our church. A handful of women who were *not* close to me were feeling very free to tell me what I should stop doing or that what I was doing was wrong: "You shouldn't travel so much. What about your kids? How's your relationship with your husband?" (If you're close with me, go ahead and ask these questions on the regular; if not, go ahead and ask your close friends these questions.) In this season of my life, I was in relational turmoil with a couple of women in my world, on the verge of a physical burnout, and going to dramatic places in my thought life, ready to be done sharing my heart with another female again. I was done inviting her (whoever she may be) in to be my friend so she could just up and leave while crushing me in the process. Anyone see now why we need to avoid the drama? It usually starts within us, and that's coming straight from the drama queen herself! I would never implore you to do anything I wasn't willing to do myself. *This mama needs to break up with drama* and own her life! Every. Day. And yes, we will get to that chapter.

The friend from the start of this chapter who reminded me of what I said about climbing the mountain together also lovingly asked me if I remembered that season. Unfortunately, yes. Can't forget it, as much as I'd love to. It's etched in my heart, soul, emotions, and memory. And then she proceeded to ask if I thought I began self-preserving in that season as I had slowly started stepping away from my responsibilities (and purpose) in our church. Because, you know, I was writing books. I was traveling. I was important. I had the She Is Free Conference. I had four kids, everyone! I didn't have time for human interaction with people who could potentially hurt me! The same friend said, "When you travel and speak, you don't have to deal with the mess of walking with people every day, right?"

Heck yes! Perfect self-preservation plan, all wrapped up in a neat and tidy bow that looks like super-holy success to the outside world. Unless it's not holy before God.

I am not belittling my calling here, and I feel strongly from the Holy Spirit that I need to make that clear. I am called to Liberty Church *and* the greater church body. Part of my purpose *is* to write, travel, speak, and invest outside of the church my husband and I were called to plant. But I have a responsibility to manage that tension in my life in a healthy way. I have to pay attention to the times when I begin to self-preserve instead of laying my life down in holy surrender.

In that particular season, it was a slippery slope that looked right, felt right, and honestly at the time *was* right. I was doing a lot of good work, but I needed a holy chiropractic adjustment to walk in alignment again. I had veered off course. I'm not supposed to stop parenting, writing, speaking, leading, and all the things, but I'm also not meant to hide behind them so that I can live a life void of meaningful, messy connection. That was *my* problem and one that only I can take responsibility for.

To avoid drama and create authentic connection in friendship, we have to be aware of our weaknesses and be vulnerable enough to bring someone in on that journey. What we don't know about ourselves can hurt us, and others. I know that this vulnerable heart likes to go all in, deep and quick, and has unknowingly welcomed in some unsafe people and learned that the hard way. I know that this causes me to become a fortress for a season so that I can heal until I'm ready to put my heart on the line again, hopefully with more wisdom.

What do you know about yourself? And who do you need to allow close enough to tell you what you *don't* know about yourself?

I need to be authentically me, and so do you if we're going to be real friends. I need to be able to come to the table as *this* mess, you know, the scary one I mentioned up above, but also willing to not *stay* this mess. I need you to receive me *and* challenge me to be better—to do better. I need you to give me some truth in love, not truth for the sake of being right and putting me in my place. I need to know I am loved before I can receive the truth from you. I need you to remind me to be me. To sit at the feet of Jesus and receive His love because I am loved—just because—even when I'm a mess. And I need to be able to reciprocate all of this to you too.

Intimacy with Jesus Takes Us out of Unholy Isolation

Friends, self-preservation is willfully choosing the pain of isolation over the potential of messy godly connection.

Okay, yes, but how do we grow to a place where our first instinct is to dive into healthy connection instead of running away from it? I've learned that the healthier I've become in my intimate relationship with Jesus, the freer I've become in friendship, and in any relationship for that matter. I stop looking to people to meet needs that they will never be able to meet in their humanness. Intimacy is simply "close familiarity or friendship; closeness."[1] I have to live from a place of being loved, not trying to scrape up and scrounge for love wherever I can find it. Being loved, receiving genuine love, is a legitimate human need, and we have to learn how to meet that need with the right thing. We can't love our neighbor and uncomplicate the friendships we are in if we don't even love our own company. And the way we begin to enjoy our own company is to receive love from the One who created us. The One whose image and likeness we are created in.

"Love the Lord your God with all your heart and with all your soul and with all your mind and with all your strength." The second is this: *"Love your neighbor as yourself."* There is no commandment greater than these. (Mark 12:30–31)

Then God said, "Let us make mankind *in our image, in our likeness,* so that they may rule over the fish in the sea and the birds in the sky, over the livestock and all the wild animals, and over all the creatures that move along the ground."

So God created mankind in his own image,
in the image of God he created them;
male and female he created them. (Gen. 1:26–27)

So, we are to love others as we love ourselves, and what's not to love when we are created in the image of a loving God?

You may scoff depending on what you've been through or if the relational trauma you've faced has affected how you see yourself, but when we become intimately aware of how wonderfully we are created (Ps. 139:13–18), it changes everything. We ourselves are triune beings, spirit, soul, and body, created in the image of a triune God who is three in one. Did you catch God's words when He said to create mankind in "our" image, in "our" likeness? We are beautifully complex. We cannot negate nor neglect the needs our spirit, soul, and body each have to be made whole. But we also cannot expect humans to meet needs that only intimacy with the Godhead can.

My husband and I have a wise counselor in our lives who has been there for us in various pivotal seasons. I recall one of the times we met with him when I was angry, hurt, tired, insecure, and isolating. He began to tell us of his morning routine and that the first thing he does is say hello to God with an awareness that he is a favorite son. So, first thing, before he reaches for his phone or Bible, before he swings his feet over the side of the bed and onto the floor, he receives the unrelenting, unceasing, unstoppable love of God. And then he begins the rest of his day with an awareness of how deeply loved he really is. It's simple, but it's a practical change we can make on a daily basis.

I can categorically say that I am a different person when I receive from God before I try to give to *or* receive from another human created in the likeness of God. My motives are in check, and I become aware of the needs of myself and others. I stop self-isolating and self-protecting and instead lean in to God's love and step into friendship with healthy expectations.

As I talked to a friend about writing this book, she told me she had been working toward intentional friendship on a regular basis with a small group of women. At one point a few years in, she began to realize she wasn't sharing as intimately, nor baring her heart as vulnerably, as the rest of the group was, and she had to be honest with them as to why. Years prior, she had been in another small group of friends. At a certain stage, those friendships began to break down and she was accused of things that simply weren't true. The damage from that caused her great pain. She realized that getting her walls to come down with her new group of friends was going to take some time and that being honest about this was necessary for her to move forward. She recognized that she was isolating and self-preserving, even in the presence of others, and she acknowledged it in a safe space before it became detrimental. She intentionally chose the potential of messy godly connection over the pain of isolation.

A reminder before we pause and reflect together: *we are not stuck*—no matter our past, no matter what a pastor, a prominent female, our spouse, or any negative voice has told us! Be honest with where you are but choose not to stay there.

REFLECTION POINTS

- Ask yourself, *Why do I isolate myself from others?*
- If we are to love our neighbor as we love ourselves, we have to be intentional to receive love from the right source first. Consider creating space in your calendar to just be. To soak. Sit. Listen. Receive. You may need to simply start with five minutes during your day and extend from there.
- Turn on a worship song. Ask a few questions of the Holy Spirit and just listen. Have a journal ready to

write down what you hear, sense, or ponder. If you're looking for love and affirmation, the presence of God is the best place to receive them first.

- Activate the truth of the Word in your life. Put it up somewhere, read it, say it, ask questions about it, wrestle with it, and let it give you life.

When I was newly saved, I read Psalm 139 and sobbed with joy and wonder. I couldn't believe how deeply I was seen or how my every need, thought, motive, longing, hope, dream, and fear could be intimately known by the God who knit me together in my mother's womb so He could have a relationship with me. I run back to this psalm, time and time again, when I look to another fallible human to give me something they are unable to give. I come back to this Scripture to be reminded of my humanity and God's great love for me.

I know I have already shared parts of this Scripture with you in previous chapters, but take some time and crack open your own Bible, read it, underline it, and take in the fullness of it. Let it restore you and remind you of who you are so that you can step into deeper wholeness. As you read it, notice what's illuminated to you. What speaks to you? What frustrates you or even makes you angry? What don't you understand? What do you understand? Do you feel like you're able to receive the truth, or do you still need certain verses to become lived revelation?

Psalm 139
> For the director of music. Of David. A psalm.
> You have searched me, LORD,
>   and you know me.

You know when I sit and when I rise;
    you perceive my thoughts from afar.
You discern my going out and my lying down;
    you are familiar with all my ways.
Before a word is on my tongue
    you, LORD, know it completely.
You hem me in behind and before,
    and you lay your hand upon me.
Such knowledge is too wonderful for me,
    too lofty for me to attain.

Where can I go from your Spirit?
    Where can I flee from your presence?
If I go up to the heavens, you are there;
    if I make my bed in the depths, you are there.
If I rise on the wings of the dawn,
    if I settle on the far side of the sea,
even there your hand will guide me,
    your right hand will hold me fast.
If I say, "Surely the darkness will hide me
    and the light become night around me,"
even the darkness will not be dark to you;
    the night will shine like the day,
    for darkness is as light to you.

For you created my inmost being;
    you knit me together in my mother's womb.
I praise you because I am fearfully and wonderfully
    made;
    your works are wonderful,
    I know that full well.
My frame was not hidden from you
    when I was made in the secret place,
    when I was woven together in the depths of the
        earth.

Your eyes saw my unformed body;
    all the days ordained for me were written in your
      book
    before one of them came to be.
How precious to me are your thoughts, God!
    How vast is the sum of them!
Were I to count them,
    they would outnumber the grains of sand—
    when I awake, I am still with you.

If only you, God, would slay the wicked!
    Away from me, you who are bloodthirsty!
They speak of you with evil intent;
    your adversaries misuse your name.
Do I not hate those who hate you, LORD,
    and abhor those who are in rebellion against you?
I have nothing but hatred for them;
    I count them my enemies.
Search me, God, and know my heart;
    test me and know my anxious thoughts.
See if there is any offensive way in me,
    and lead me in the way everlasting.

Chapter 5

IT'S TIME TO BREAK UP
WITH DRAMA

You can always tell who the strong women are. They
are the ones building one another up rather than tearing
each other down.

Unknown

So, I downloaded a Who Unfollowed Me app, for like, thirty
minutes because, apparently, I don't need anyone else in my
life to create drama for me; I'm pretty good at doing it on
my own. I have to say, my curiosity, insecurity, and general
desire to be liked got the best of me for a hot second, as they
do on occasion.

Worst. Idea. Ever.

These "Who the heck would unfollow *me*?" apps are really
great at breeding drama in your head and heart because you
begin to create imaginary scenarios as to why people unfollowed you. You envision melodramatic future conversations

in which you will confront and talk to said unfollower and ask them why they left your entourage. I mean, how could they?

The honest-to-God truth is, they were probably never your actual friend in the first place—and, logically, I'm pretty sure we know that. Yet, why do we need "them" to like us? Follow us? Affirm us? Agree with us? What is it in our human nature that craves attention, affection, and affirmation in unhealthy ways, and if we don't get it, drama ensues?

This chapter is going to be a little bit different from the others. Throughout each section, I'll give you some keys to breaking up with drama in your life and we'll also have some time to pause and reflect together. So, here are the first two keys:

Key #1: Locate (because they already exist) some friends in real life (not on social media) who won't unfollow you, no matter how hard or dark things get. Don't focus on the ones that aren't with you; focus on the ones that are.

Key #2: Consider how you can intentionally break unhealthy thought patterns and cycles in your life. What does this practically look like for you on a daily basis? How can you start today (i.e., deleting/never downloading or ever using "Who unfollowed me?" apps)? And as a rule of thumb, usually our real friends will stick around to see us through the changes we're making—*if* we're willing to change. If we're not willing to change, even our real friends will set boundaries with us.

Now, why did I use the word *locate* in key #1? Because I would go so far as to say that you have good friends who already exist. Maybe you're just not focusing on them or being intentional with them because you're so caught up in the drama of those "friends" who are *not* for you or are sucking the life out of you. Why do I say this? Unfortunately, because of personal experience. I can get so caught up in thinking about those who aren't for me or don't like me, fabricating what they must be thinking or saying about me, that I forget the faithful friends who have always been there and who keep showing up. I miss out on opportunities to create new, healthy memories with real-life, present friends.

My best friend of twenty-plus years, Tanya, and I had an honest conversation on a long drive together. We took an autopsy of a difficult season in our friendship when we "broke up" and went our separate ways for almost a year. Disagreement, misunderstanding, and unspoken expectations of one another brought division to our relationship. We eventually confronted the issues we were facing, reconciled, healed, and began to rebuild our friendship. I actually write about it in my book *Fake or Follower*.

Proverbs 27:6 says, "Wounds from a sincere friend are better than many kisses from an enemy" (NLT). On that drive, Tanya got candid with me as only a true friend can. She reminded me that through the years of our friendship, she had felt uncomfortable and uneasy on several occasions about some "friends" who tried to enter my world. She had lovingly warned me, but nine times out of ten, I didn't listen to her advice. I would defend the person and my relationship with them, and then either the relationship would fall apart, drama would ensue, or I would face betrayal and pain, and yet Tanya never said, "I told you so." Instead, she patiently waited for me to come back. But the less I trusted her wisdom, discernment, and warning, the more she pulled away from me and our friendship, because fractures in our trust with one another had appeared, and the honest parts of our relationship had become one-sided. My actions kept saying to her, "You'll wait for me. I *won't* listen to you or your wisdom, but be my friend, even when I treat you like garbage."

Well, thank God she didn't leave. But I needed to repent for devaluing her and the years of investment and love she'd poured into me. And she repented for stepping back instead of stepping in when I diminished her input—even though I can see why she did. Not only did we repent and make amends; we chose to make changes. To turn toward each other and continue to have hard conversations whenever we need to.

As we talked during this long drive, we both had this revelation: "It's not the person; it's the pattern." What do I mean by that? The problem wasn't the person who stepped in to be in a relationship with me; it was the pattern I operated in. We all operate in cyclical patterns if we don't get understanding on *what* they are and *how* to break them by walking through healing with Jesus and setting new boundaries to create a healthier pattern. My unconscious pattern was one of trying to receive affirmation from particular people who told me I was special, that they needed me, that I was awesome, gifted, and worthy of their love. Often, these people appeared to be spiritually superior to me, possessing the ability to prophesy and speak mysteries accurately over my life, which seemed to meet a felt need of mine. But as time passed, it would seem their motive wasn't love (see 1 Cor. 13:2). I felt seen and known until the tables turned and things began to fall apart. Then I'd go running back to Tanya to talk. Frankly, I didn't even know I had been doing this until the damage was done to a faithful, lifelong friendship with someone who chose to stick around and tell me the truth, even when it hurt.

To break cycles and patterns in our lives, we have to stop conforming to the ways or patterns of the world (repent) and then think and live differently (make a choice). Romans 12:2 says, "Do not conform to the pattern of this world, but be transformed by the renewing of your mind. Then you will be able to test and approve what God's will is—his good, pleasing and perfect will." I need to stop the negative cyclical thinking and living within me, and to do this, I must choose the pain of change over the pain of staying the same. What unhealthy patterns do you operate in? Where do you need to repent and make different small-yet-effective choices daily? Which friendships do you need to be intentional with?

We're going to hit a few heavy topics in this chapter: gossip, games, insecurity, jealousy, competition, catastrophizing, and self-sabotage. But before we dive in, let's look to the Bible, a book that's *literally* full of drama, which points to our desperate need for Jesus.

Drama and Our Desperate Need for Jesus

It seems to me that Jesus had a high drama threshold with His disciples. First of all, He chose Peter, who . . . well . . . just makes us all feel normal in our passionate mood swings. Peter leaves everything to follow Jesus immediately after a miraculous catch of fish (Luke 5:8–11). He has the public revelation that Jesus is the Son of God (Matt. 16:16) and directly after that, Peter is called "Satan" by Jesus because he is trying to obstruct the plan of Jesus going to the cross, having in mind the concerns of man rather than the concerns of God (Matt. 16:23). Then there's Thomas. I mean, even after Jesus dies, rises again, and is standing right in front of his face, he basically says to the Son of God in regard to His death and resurrection, "Prove it." Jesus, in His deep love for Thomas, does prove it by showing him His scars (John 20:24–29). And then there are the squabbles among the disciples about who's the greatest (Matt 18:1–4; Mark 9:33–36; Luke 9:46–47), not just once but even at the Last Supper when Jesus is trying to intimately connect with them over a meal for the last time and usher them into the new covenant. Luke 22:24 says, "A dispute also arose among them as to which of them was considered to be greatest." Jesus reminds them once again that whoever wants to be the greatest is the one who becomes a servant of all. Oh, and let's not forget that at the Last Supper, Jesus publicly calls out His betrayer while the disciples "question among themselves"—that is, gossip about—"which of them it might be who would do this" (22:21–23). And Jesus doesn't hold back with Peter either, who, in what appears to be an extreme swing for the fences, making sure everyone knows he's *not* the betrayer, shouts (well, as I read it, I imagine he shouts), "Lord, I am ready to go with you to prison and to death" (22:33). Jesus tells Peter that by the next morning (when the rooster crows), he will have denied that he ever knew Jesus, not just once, but three times. Drama, drama, and more drama. I mean, even after this very melodramatic last meal together, Jesus *needs* His three closest friends to watch and pray with Him in the garden during His darkest hour before He goes to His death, and He finds them sleeping (22:39–46).

That's just a snippet of some of the interactions Jesus had with His twelve disciples—the people He *chose* to walk in close relationship with. Jesus shows us that He doesn't let drama slip by; He addresses it head-on and sometimes it gets awkward. He doesn't ignore it; He speaks to it. He knows it's a part of the human story, but it doesn't get to dominate the conversation or have the last word. We see mood swings, dramatic statements, mistrust, insecurity, comparison, competition, gossip, games, jealousy, and apathy, and those are just in what I mentioned above. So, if Jesus had drama all around Him and addressed and walked *through* it, so can we. To have uncomplicated friendships, avoid the drama, and begin to create authentic connection, we have to keep Jesus right in the center of it all.

Green Rooms, Gossip, and Games

People get weird in green rooms. Like, forget they're a regular human who poops, farts, and picks their nose on a daily basis sort of weird. Why can't we just be normal?

I have a good friend who is down to earth—so down to earth you wouldn't believe this story is about her. She happened to be invited into a green room at a Christian gathering (which sounds like an oxymoron) to hang with a "famous" Christian band. She was totally normal until the lead singer walked into the room, and then it happened. She grabbed his hand and shook it repeatedly without letting go while introducing herself with fervor and passion: her first name, middle name, second middle name, and last name, her job title, her church, and basically what she wanted to name all her future children (okay, that last part is a lie). Then she just stood there. After a long and awkward pause while looking into his eyes, she said, "Goodbye," while she walked backward toward the door to exit the green room. All other conversation had ceased, every eye glued to this uncomfortable yet entertaining interaction. The icing on the cake of this story is that, before she walked out of the room, she took the last moment of this already amazingly embarrassing moment, put her hand to her forehead, and proceeded to salute the lead singer.

I tell you all of this to ask you, what is your figurative "green room" in life? Where do you lose your identity, get all awkward, and start acting like someone else? We can't ever truly uncomplicate our friendships if we don't get to be us, but we also can't blame the green room (the environment or situation) for *why* we can't be ourselves. Yes, sometimes we actually need to make the hard call and leave or change the environment we keep putting ourselves in, because its ecosystem isn't healthy or life-giving. A homogeneous culture (or relationship) where you have to assimilate or conform to fit in is dangerous. The green room is simply an illustration. It's a reminder that we step into different environments all the time, positive and negative, but who will we be in those moments? Will we live congruently with our God-given identity, even if we're not seen as cool or good enough? Will we choose integrity over image? Out of the abundance of the heart, the underlying issues of life, the mouth speaks (Prov. 4:23; Luke 6:45). Also, some people in some environments will never be your friend, and that's okay. Stop creating false worlds and friendships in your mind that were never meant for your destiny.

I've been in green rooms with people who *used to be* some of my greatest role models, and I have been crushed as I watched and listened to them act and live differently behind the scenes from what they preached on a platform. I've heard gossip and slander that was never meant for my ears and have been in the middle of unhealthy games that I never asked to be in, all in "godly" green rooms, and it shattered my heart. But the Lord reminded me that I am not subject to environments, gossip, or games. I get to choose my response. I get to choose my friends. And I get to choose who I will be—real, down-to-earth, I-am-who-He-says-I-am Andi or shallow, enter-into-the-gossip-and-games, make-me-feel-sick-to-my-stomach Andi. It's a slippery slope.

This is not about throwing anyone under the bus; this is about us looking at *our* own hearts and choosing to avoid drama, because as long as we're on earth, we'll be faced with the option to be or not to be drawn into slander, gossip, and games in church circles (I hate that this is true), social media platforms, dinner tables, small groups, family gatherings, friendship circles, and any scenario where human beings are present. Proverbs 6:16–19 is clear:

> There are six things the LORD hates,
>   seven that are detestable to him:
>   haughty eyes,
>   *a lying tongue*,
>   hands that shed innocent blood,
>   a heart that devises wicked schemes,
>   feet that are quick to rush into evil,
>   *a false witness who pours out lies*
>   *and a person who stirs up conflict in the community.*

I pay attention when the Lord says He *hates* something, and I make a willful choice to *run* in the opposite direction of it. I have definitely been the target of the above list that the Lord hates, and unfortunately, I've knowingly engaged in hurting others with my words and in other things that break the heart of God and bring disunity. Yet at the same time, I have a healthy fear of God—who is just in all His ways—knowing that I will answer to Him at the end of my life for every word that leaves my mouth, and I try not to voluntarily entangle myself with the things He hates. And when I do knowingly ensnare myself in gossip, games, lies, and slander, I am quick to repent to God and others who may have been present. We may think it's much easier to point the finger at someone else to explain away why we are living the way we're living, doing the things we're doing, or saying the things we're saying, *but we are more powerful than that.* Free will is a gift from God, and we get to choose what (and whom) we align with.

So, don't become someone different just because the environment changes. Be the awkward, unchanged person in the room who brings conviction by not entering into the games. Don't enter into gossip, slander, and conversations that degrade or hurt others. As a matter of fact, hit these head-on like Jesus would, with questions or comments like "Have you talked to that person yet about what you're telling me?" or "I feel uncomfortable talking about them when they're not here." Go ahead and call gossips and slanderers lovingly to the carpet. The apostle Paul had no qualms about doing so, and we all know that saying nothing is also saying something.

> *Do not let any unwholesome talk come out of your mouths*, but only what is helpful for building others up according to their needs, that it may benefit those who listen. And do not grieve the Holy Spirit of God, with whom you were sealed for the day of redemption. *Get rid of all bitterness, rage and anger, brawling and slander, along with every form of malice.* Be kind and compassionate to one another, forgiving each other, just as in Christ God forgave you. (Eph. 4:29–32)

And don't enter into games. I've felt like a pawn, stuck in the middle of situations I never asked to be in, and it was damaging to relationships on all sides. Maybe the damage is already done, maybe you were thrust in the middle and never asked to be there, but advocate for yourself and stop the drama, even if it means severing an unhealthy relationship or two. And as a rule, if you're not willing to say something to someone's face, maybe don't say it to anyone else but Jesus.

Contend for peace, love, and unity. Walk in your God-given identity as an example to others, no matter what goes on around you, and call others to rise to the challenge as well.

In Philippians 4:2–3, Paul pleads with Euodia and Syntyche, two women he has co-labored with in the gospel, to get it together. "I plead with Euodia and I plead with Syntyche to be of the same mind in the Lord. Yes, and I ask you, my true companion, help these women since they have contended at my side in the cause of the gospel, along with Clement and the rest of my co-workers, whose names are in the book of life." They are so valuable to the cause of Christ that Paul addresses them in a letter to the church of Philippi. Something was obviously going on with these two women, and even though we don't have the details, we know that they were friends on mission together, and it mattered that they sorted out their issues to advance the gospel.

I guess in reality this is the point. There are bigger issues at hand than our personal drama, and we need to realign with purpose and godly friendships to live on mission.

Okay, so here is the third key to breaking up with drama in your life:

Key #3: Choose honesty (with yourself and others) and integrity over games and image. Self-reflect to see where you've been complicit in gossip, slander, or games. Where do you need to be powerful and repent, apologize, or make things right? Where do you need to stop blaming environments (aka the green rooms of life or the church you went to or your work environment) for why you act the way you act? You don't need this drama in your life, and you can take ownership of, change, and/or step away from unhealthy ecosystems. You are powerful enough to make things right—don't wait for someone else to make the first move.

Insecurity, Jealousy, and Competition

Just a few little things that we don't ever deal with, right? I wish. Insecurity, jealousy, and competition all go hand in hand.

Insecurity: uncertainty or anxiety about oneself; lack of confidence.[1]

Jealousy: [the state of] feeling or showing envy of someone or their achievements and advantages.[2]

Competition: [the act of] striving against one another to gain or win something.[3]

All of the above stem from core identity issues and, I will say, flourish in environments that allow and perpetuate them. When we don't know who we are, we lack confidence to walk in our God-given identity (because we don't even know what it is) and begin to operate from a place of insecurity. We don't know our place or our worth and therefore lack confidence to be us, whether we are meek and mild, demonstrative and outgoing, or some other wonderful combination created in the image of God. Then we begin to envy those we perceive to be better off than us. We begin to want what they have instead of looking at what we already have. We stop seeking God's unique purpose for us and look to others to affirm who we are (or who we wish we were) and tell us what we're called to do. We become aware of the ways we don't seem to measure up to societal standards. We continually fall short and just can't

98

seem to get what so-and-so got, even though we should have because we're just as qualified—if not more so. And before we know it, we're in competition with our sisters, trying to one-up them instead of cheering them on.

None of us wants to be here, but we've all found ourselves in these dramatic spaces in life from time to time. It's hard to uncomplicate our friendships when we don't know who we are and everyone we meet is a potential rival rather than a potential sister or friend.

When my husband was discipled years ago, one of his mentors told him that we are prone to open a door of sin in our lives when we are operating from a place of "HALTS"—meaning, when we are Hurt, Angry, Lonely, Tired, or Stressed. We are probably at least one of those things, if not more, on any given day. Why do I tell you this? Consider using HALTS as a dashboard for when you are more prone to stirring up drama. When we don't check our drama meter regularly, we begin to affirm our own decision to sin. In the cold, hard light of day, we have to come to grips with the truth that *it is* a sin to not love who we are created to be. And I'm not talking about weird self-worship here, because that's a sin in and of itself (Prov. 18:12; 2 Tim. 3:1–2). Popular culture has way too much to say about what we should look and act like, when our Creator enjoyed creating us and loves being with us—every shape, size, color, and personality that we are uniquely fashioned to be. He also wants to remind us of who we are and what we are created for. But that comes with a choice on our end to turn to Him instead of others to affirm our identity. When we begin to insult the Sculptor's work (look in the mirror; I'm talking about you), we begin to operate in envy and jealousy of others, which is also a sin. Then we begin to compete with our brothers and sisters in Christ for our place, which, yes, is also a sin.

Don't believe me? Here's a biblical perspective.

Then I observed that *most people are motivated to success because they envy their neighbors.* But this, too, is meaningless— like chasing the wind. (Eccles. 4:4 NLT)

Ask yourself, *What's my motivation to succeed? God's purpose or selfish purposes?*

Pay careful attention to your own work, for then you will get the satisfaction of a job well done, and you won't need to *compare yourself to anyone else.* (Gal. 6:4 NLT)

Ask yourself, *Am I paying attention to the good work that's in front of me or comparing my outcomes to other people's outcomes?*

But who are you, a human being, to talk back to God? "Shall what is formed say to the one who formed it, *'Why did you make me like this?'"* Does not the potter have the right to make out of the same lump of clay some pottery for special purposes and some for common use? (Rom. 9:20–21)

Ask yourself, *Am I questioning why God made me the way He did and why He is using me the way He does? Or am I running in my lane with godly contentment?*

And he said to them, *"You are those who justify yourselves before men, but God knows your hearts.* For what is exalted among men is an abomination in the sight of God." (Luke 16:15 ESV)

Ask yourself, *Am I living a life justified before God or justified before men? Do I feel the need to say things to justify myself, or do I trust that God is my vindicator?*

Do nothing from selfish ambition or conceit, but in humility count others more significant than yourselves. Let each of you look not only to his own interests, but also to the interests of others. (Phil. 2:3–4 ESV)

Ask yourself, *Am I doing this to be seen as gifted, talented, or better than (insert name), or am I looking to others' interests and abilities and cheering them on?*

Now the works of the flesh are evident: sexual immorality, impurity, sensuality, idolatry, sorcery, enmity, strife, *jealousy,* fits of anger, *rivalries, dissensions, divisions. (Gal. 5:19–20 ESV)*

Ask yourself, *Am I operating in the works of the flesh (jealousy, rivalry, anger, division, etc.) or in the fruit of the Spirit— love, joy, peace, patience, kindness, goodness, faithfulness, gentleness, and self-control?*

Breaking up with drama starts with breaking unhealthy agreements in our own hearts, where we let insecurity, jealousy, justification, competition, and ultimately pride take root, germinate, and multiply until they bear ugly fruit. Tending to the soil of our hearts is not a one-time job; it's a daily discipline and a lifelong journey.

What about Catastrophizing and Self-Sabotage?

Dr. John M. Grohol says this about catastrophizing:

Catastrophizing is an irrational thought a lot of us have in believing that something is far worse than it actually is. Catastrophizing can generally take two different forms: making a catastrophe out of a current situation and imagining making a catastrophe out of a future situation.[4]

Take a moment and look at your current friendships and relationships. Are you overdramatizing (i.e., making a catastrophe out of a current situation)? Look at it rationally. It is really that bad? Are you taking ten steps forward and imagining possible future catastrophic outcomes in your current friendships and relationships? Catastrophizing starts in our thought life and begins to build momentum depending on where we allow those thoughts to go. If we don't take them captive, we cause them to become our reality. Remember Romans 12:2? "Do not conform to the pattern of this world, but be transformed by the renewing of your mind. Then you will be able to test and approve what God's will is—his good, pleasing and perfect will." When we get a handle on our thought life, we are then able to "test and approve what God's will is" for any situation in our lives instead of meditating on potential disasters.

To intentionally uncomplicate our friendships, we have to recognize when we are catastrophizing a situation or circumstance that isn't a catastrophe at all. We have to be honest with where the friendship or relationship is truly at and what it's becoming rather than letting fear from past brokenness in female relationships cause us to catastrophize and, in turn, self-sabotage and ruin the relationship or make it fall apart— sometimes before it even starts. Often, this is a subconscious behavior, but I would encourage you to look back and take stock of your behavior in past relationships. Do you see a pattern of catastrophizing and self-sabotage? If yes, ask yourself and the Holy Spirit, "What is the truth?" Ask someone you trust to sort out your thoughts with you. This is especially helpful if you're having a hard time looking at certain situations and relationships rationally. When you speak them out loud, you may recognize the lies you're believing before the person you confide in even gets to tell you what they observe. When you receive the truth, consider writing it down and speaking it out loud to stop irrational thoughts that lead to catastrophizing.

My husband helps me with this all the time. Here's an example: In the middle of COVID-19, we were having Zoom meetings left, right, and center with our team, as was the rest of the world. It was a difficult time, and everyone was out of sorts—in all honesty, probably walking through one of the stages of grief. In the middle of a meeting with our Liberty online team, I broke down crying like I had just gotten the news that someone died. I was so embarrassed but couldn't stop, so I got up and excused myself from the meeting. Immediately, I started catastrophizing in my thoughts: *I'm sure the team thinks I'm a child. I bet they disrespect me. I know they're talking about me and how emotional I am. I think I should step aside. Maybe I'm not created to lead with Paul. I've lost their respect. That's it, I'm done.* The next morning, I basically said all those things out loud to Paul, and with his steady love and zero sarcasm, he said, "None of that is true. And if they do think that way, too bad. You're a great leader. Don't take yourself out of the race." Unemotional, rational truth. He hit the catastrophizing, self-sabotaging nail on the head. It can be done; it just takes a conscious effort.

For me, again, a lot of my catastrophizing, self-sabotage, and self-rejection go back to attachment issues, from which God is consistently healing me when they come to the surface. I love that at the right time, in the right season, He is always willing and able to heal us of all brokenness.

REFLECTION POINTS

- **Insecurity:** Ask God who you are as a creation made in His image. Write it down. Speak it out loud. Let Psalm 139 be your true north. Find friends who remind you who you truly are, not who they think you should be.

- **Jealousy:** Ask yourself why you're jealous. What do you believe you lack that causes you to envy another person? What has God already given you? Write it down and begin to thank God out loud with sincere appreciation for what you have and who you are.

- **Competition:** What lie have you believed that made you think you have to compete for your place in this race called life? What situation or person made you feel this way? Who, or what organization, do you need to possibly forgive for cultivating an environment of competition? Why do you have to diminish another's life to feel important? Or do better than them to be successful? Ask God to give you the truth in place of that lie. Receive it and begin to walk in it.

- **Catastrophizing:** What relationships or scenarios, past or present, are you dramatizing (aka catastrophizing)? What is the truth? Let go of the catastrophic scenario you've built up in your head and heart. Repent of your ways and worship God for being present in your life right here, right now.

- **Self-Sabotage:** What relationships are you currently sabotaging but have been unaware that you're doing so? What do you need to do in this specific scenario to stop? What is one practical thing you can do today to stop the self-sabotage?

The Root of It All: Fear of Man (or Woman)

I believe that fear is the enemy's greatest weapon because it is the exact opposite of the nature and character of God, who is *love*. And we know this truth (whether it has dropped down into our hearts as revelation is the question): *perfect love casts out all fear, because fear has to do with punishment* (1 John 4:18). So, where are we allowing punishment to govern our lives? Where does it exist in our friendships or relationships? Maybe you punish yourself because you don't feel you deserve such a beautiful friendship. Maybe you bring punishment into the friendship to see if that person will stick around, even when you hold them at arm's length. God wants you to turn to Him and receive His true, undying, unending, unyielding love so that you can learn the difference between what you *think* you (or they) deserve and what He freely gives, even though none of us "deserve" it—His pure love. Remember, intimacy with Jesus takes us out of unholy isolation from others. Isolation is a self-protection mechanism that manifests when we believe we (or they) deserve punishment.

Friend, I can't encourage you enough to let His healing love in.

And can I just say this? Please stop creating false, fantasy friendships that can never exist in the real world and only lead to disappointment. Genuine, honest, gritty, reciprocal friendships are completely imperfect, messy, and beautiful.

How do we face fear and break up with drama in our lives? Here is the fourth key:

Key #4: Maybe it's time to unfollow and break up with fear. Ask yourself why you come into agreement with fear and punish yourself or others in relationships rather than letting love heal and lead the way.

Radical Ownership

One last thought before we dive into creating authentic connection. How do we break up with drama on a daily basis? *Take radical ownership of our own drama*—the stuff we create, make up in our heads, and stir up. It's simple, but here's where I'll finish the "break up with drama" chapter. You have to *own your life, your story, your actions*, drama included. Stop blaming others for why things are the way they are. Remember how powerful you are; you can step away from toxic environments, relationships, and circles. You can make changes within yourself and with your daily rhythms starting today.

And here ends the "break up with drama" lesson with our fifth key:

> *Key #5:* Own your life. Your story. Your drama—the stuff you created and the drama you find yourself in. Cry out and search for wisdom about what to do next, and then obediently do it. Don't just be a hearer and a reader of the Word; become a doer of the Word, no matter the cost.

part 2

UNCOMPLICATING
ALL THE THINGS

chapter 6

NO, YOU GO FIRST

The only way to have a friend is to be one.

Ralph Waldo Emerson

Now we pivot.

The first half of this book was all about identifying heart issues, unhealthy cycles, and the internal and external drama that holds us back from entering into genuine friendship. Now it's time to intentionally uncomplicate things, create authentic connection, and walk *together* to fulfill our purpose in God-given community. And sometimes, even when we'd like someone else to pave the way for us in doing all of the above, we have to choose to go *first* and carve out a path—otherwise we may be waiting for a while, even forever.

We've learned together that fundamental ownership of one's life changes everything and is a building block to authentic connection. Often, the *cost* of that ownership, though, accompanied by intentional investment into meaningful connection, means that we'll have to go first when we just wish someone else would. It means that when we hope and pray that the offender in a relationship will acknowledge their fault, say sorry, or do the right thing, usually the onus lands back on us to do the right thing *first*, even if they never do.

As I sat across the table from a good friend at our "last supper" (okay, it was brunch *with* carbs) before she moved out of town, we talked about all the things. There were awkward, loud tears, with exchanges of "I love you" and "I'm going to miss you so much" as we reached across the table to hold hands (kidding—about the hand holding part that is; the rest is true and we didn't care who looked). In all the chatting, I distinctly remember asking the question, "What fills you with holy anger, like, really fires you up?" I love this question because it often points to passion and calling. She answered and then returned the question, to which I said, "People who don't own their 'stuff.' I just get so fired up when people blame others for why they are the way they are and don't take ownership of their lives." And when pastoring or leading on any front, you are the bull's-eye of blame for other people's problems, so I'm fired up a lot.

Like I said at the end of chapter 5, the only way we change is to own our lives, our stories, our drama. The drama we find ourselves in and the drama we create. One of the key ways we can resolve issues in our lives or relationships is to acknowledge and own our part of the story. And yes, I'll say it again: *choosing* to go first when we wish somebody else would.

Sometimes we have to choose to forgive and say sorry first, even if it's never returned. Other times, we choose to go first to give grace when all we want to do is judge, blame, put up walls, and cut people off. Sometimes we choose to go first to set boundaries and *spoken* expectations when we'd rather passive-aggressively let the lines fall where they may or dismiss people who are boundaryless and get all up in our physical, mental, and emotional space, expecting too much of us. Other times, we choose to go first in making peace with one another (not *keeping* the peace; that's different—sweeping things under the carpet only hides a mess that you'll have to deal with later), which is disruptive because hard conversations usually happen when it's time to make peace. And yes, sometimes we choose to go first in setting others free because an essential ending has come in a friendship. It's painful, it's hard, but it can bring life and freedom to both parties if it is the right thing to do.

So, let's dig in, shall we? This is an invitation to do the right thing and go first, even when our human nature wants someone else to fix the issue at hand instead.

Go First to Forgive and Say Sorry

I've been married for almost twenty years now, and I still hardly ever want to be the first to say sorry to my husband. When Tanya and I weren't doing well in our friendship, as I referenced in the last chapter, I had all the reasons why she needed to go first and apologize. I can be quick with comebacks in a fight, so I knew I could come out on top if we went head-to-head in an argument. On reflection, seeing my pride is a hard pill to swallow.

Anyone else feel like the apostle Paul when it comes to being at war with our flesh and selfish human nature? He says, "I do not understand what I do. For what I want to do I do not do, but what I hate I do" (Rom. 7:15). Now, is anyone else dying to know what Paul was wrestling with here? I mean, I want to sit down with him and ask what it was that

111

he just kept doing and couldn't stop doing. And why couldn't he stop?

Let's look through the lens of this verse when it comes to forgiveness. Do you wrestle with this? Do you find yourself getting bitter and angry and going inside of yourself instead of going first to extend love and forgiveness, repeating patterns you wish you would stop repeating? If love truly is patient and kind, doesn't envy or boast, and isn't proud . . . if love genuinely isn't self-seeking or easily angered and doesn't hold a record of wrongs (1 Cor. 13:4–8), then what does that mean for us? How should we respond to conflict, pain, differences of opinion, and discord? I hate to say that I am superior at holding a record of wrongs—and I really wish I wasn't. Is anyone else with me? And my judgmental, self-righteous pride gets in the way of choosing to go first, every single time. This is my struggle and it's ugly, but what is yours? How can we *own* our shortfalls, intentionally invite the Holy Spirit in, and then begin to change?

When it comes to loving another person, what part of 1 Corinthians 13:4–8 is your biggest hurdle to going first? If you can name it, you can overcome it.

- Is it *patience* with friends who never listen, keep doing the same thing over and over again, and never "get it" (whatever "it" is)? patience c my man.
- Is *kindness* your hurdle, (when sarcasm) selfishness, self-righteousness, pride, a harsh word, or indifference that stems from the depths of your heart bubbles out of your mouth or manifests in your actions?
- Do you find yourself *envious* of what others have achieved and therefore begin *boasting* about what you It does not bother me at all.

have achieved to inflate your own self-worth, because insecurity is lurking where it shouldn't be?

- Does *pride* stop you in your tracks from reaching out first, because you just can't humble yourself to believe that you could be wrong too? *NO NOT AT ALL*

- Do you make everything about you, *seeking self* instead of lifting your eyes off of yourself to consider the feelings of others? *Main problem*

- Do you explode in unholy *anger* (and call it holy) instead of submitting the entirety of your life—emotions included—to Christ so that you can extend genuine love and forgiveness? *Yes I have anger issues*

- Or, like me, is your biggest hurdle excelling at holding a *record of wrongs*, becoming bitter and refusing to move forward, all because you have a list to go back to whenever you'd like? Thank goodness God does not use the record of wrongs that He *could* use against us, because His Son, Jesus, covered all our sin. *Yes at times*

So, what's your hurdle? Our Enneagram number, DISC profile (generally, our personality type), upbringing, past friendship issues, social status, and a thousand other factors *cannot be* our perpetual excuse for why we don't change, grow, and begin to create authentic connection. Yes, those things can inform us as to why we make some of the decisions we do, but growing in maturity means that we stop allowing those things to justify our actions anymore. What I love, though, is once our personal hurdles are identified, we can begin to train ourselves through intention, passion, discipline, the power of the Holy Spirit, and renewal from the Word of God to jump over them. I have always felt that it's disempowering to only point out a problem without having a meaningful, practical way forward. And I have seen in my own life that through a combination of the Word, my free will to make different choices, the indwelling of the Holy Spirit to empower me, the choice to remain in godly community, and wise counsel from a select few, I slowly but surely keep changing, growing, and jumping over the hurdles placed in front of me.

I remember reading 1 Corinthians 6:19–20 to Sam, my youngest son, and having a meaningful conversation about it. It says, "Do you not know that your bodies are temples of the Holy Spirit, who is in you, whom you have received from God? You are not your own; you were bought at a price. Therefore honor God with your bodies." I explained to Sam how amazing this was. That the same power that raised Christ from the dead has chosen to make us His dwelling place. We are a temple, and if we live aware of that, it changes things. Sometimes I'll say to Sam, when he gets cutting and sarcastic (he's genuinely funny—but sometimes it goes too far), "Hey, who lives in you?"

And he'll say under his breath, usually with a slight eye roll, "The Holy Spirit."

To which I'll say, "Would the Holy Spirit say that?"

Another eye roll. "No . . ."

"What would the Holy Spirit say?"

And out of his mouth comes some life-giving word or sentence that changes the atmosphere.

You get the picture, right?

The evidence of the Holy Spirit dwelling within us is the fruit of the Spirit outside of us. This means that cultivating love, joy, peace, patience, kindness, goodness, faithfulness, gentleness, and self-control (Gal. 5:22–23) is what causes us to choose to go first to say sorry, ask for forgiveness, and let go whether a bridge is built or not. Maybe it's time to do a fruit check? Because we are all producing something, so what is it?

Remember this: even if you forgive, it doesn't mean that you have to or should dive right back into the relationship. And if you do, you'll have to establish a new normal. Is the person you've forgiven producing "fruit in keeping with repentance" (Luke 3:8)? If not, you can still love them from afar, set firm boundaries, and forgive as many times as you need to. But if their life lacks the fruit of repentance and ownership, you can lovingly keep your distance. Continually opening yourself up to someone who refuses to change is unwise, and you simply don't have to do that.

REFLECTION POINTS

- What's your biggest hurdle to going first in forgiving or saying you're sorry? *With my parents Its hard.*
- Choose to repent and then go first, even if forgiveness isn't reciprocated. Set your heart free to move forward. And yes, you'll probably be forgiving them from the privacy of your bedroom or prayer closet as you bring your words before God. I don't suggest writing said offender an email, posting (passively or aggressively) on social media, or sending a text to tell them why you're forgiving them. → *I turn my pain into jokes and laugh at myself*
- Forgiving someone does not automatically mean reconciliation. You may not remain in a friendship or relationship with the person you need to forgive or apologize to, but the burden you were never meant to carry will be removed from your shoulders. → *I feel like I may have burdened my friends with my negative attitude towards things I*

have at times been negative towards them and probably gave them too tough love when they needed to feel like I was on their side

Go First to Give Grace

As I chatted with my friend Dawn Sadler, an all-around boss lady, coach, and culture shaper, we talked about how grace is such a beautiful gift in friendship. Both of us, for various reasons, need to give and *receive* (a whole lot of) grace because—well, we're human. Dawn, a natural confronter who sweeps nothing under the carpet and is a fierce protector of the flock, is often misunderstood. She's an Eight on the Enneagram, which is literally called a Protective Challenger. Whereas my Four-ness is a lot to be around close-up sometimes—not always but sometimes. When I'm doing great, I'm authentic, deep, and empathetic, and I express my emotions in a balanced fashion and help others do the same. When I'm not doing well, my emotional intensity is full-of-judgment, everyone-walking-on-eggshells, sort-of-moody, and I-don't-know-where-she-hid-the-explosives scary. People generally fear for their lives. I become like a turtle who goes into her shell but who also could be holding a knife in there if you come knocking.

But no matter your personality type, how good is it when someone recognizes that you screwed up royally or simply didn't communicate with them in a way they needed you to, but they don't put you on blast, cut you off, "cancel" you, or serve you with a lengthy verbal process of all the ways you've disappointed them or hurt them? *Isn't it amazing when they give you grace instead* and recognize that you are a human being on the journey, trying to submit every part of your life to produce the right fruit? When grace is given, it's overwhelming in all the right ways. And how beautiful it is when we get to a place in our lives where we can go first to give grace even when it's not reciprocated.

Do you remember when you first received this amazing grace from Christ? Do you remember when it became real that the penalty for your sin was death? I do. I remember what it felt like to be overwhelmed by the filth I'd lived in from the choices I'd made when my back was turned to God. There's a reason why the song "Amazing Grace" says, "Amazing grace, how sweet the sound that saved a *wretch* like me." Calling oneself a wretch is harsh, cruel, and degrading, but it's in contrast to what we receive—grace—and who we become—sons and daughters. And we receive not just any kind of grace but *amazing grace*. Grace is not what we deserved for the lives we chose to live separated from God, but grace is what we were given nonetheless.

Picture with me for a moment a court of law. You are on trial for murder, you are guilty, and you know you are. There is a deep fear rumbling around in your gut because you are aware that the penalty for your transgression is death. At the end of your trial, with all the evidence pointing to your obvious guilt and the Judge's gavel swung up in midair, about to bring down judgment and sentence your life to be over, a major plot twist takes place. In a dramatic turn of events, the Judge's beloved only Son walks into the courtroom. Every eye in the room has now turned toward Him with wonder . . . "Why is He here?" The truth is, He is known in town for His spotless record, right living, love for others, and plight against injustice. He raises His voice, crying out on your behalf, and says that He'll take your place and die instead. The only stipulation is that you are to go and live free, with no burden of your past sins on your record. You are no longer charged—no longer guilty—your record is expunged, and instead, the Judge's beloved Son now carries your guilt and shame. The truth is, you don't know what to do with all these feelings. You *are* guilty. You *are* a murderer. You *should* die, but in a crazy plot twist, you have been given the *grace to live*—like, really get out there and live like your past never happened sort of *live*. That is the crazily amazing grace that doesn't make sense but that we've all been given through Christ.

But to give this grace away? That's hard. And we can't do it without Jesus. Of course, we want to be loved this way, but if we're honest and check our hearts, sometimes it's hard to go first to give this to others because they *are* guilty of transgression against us.

REFLECTION POINTS

Here are a few things to remember when choosing to go first to give grace to another:

- Someone—first and foremost Jesus, and then others— extended grace to you. Remember how that felt? Yeah, it felt good, and it allowed you to keep going in all your imperfection. It allowed you to grow. Also, remember that "*all* have sinned and fall short of the glory of God" (Rom. 3:23), you and I included. Therefore, let's have a little grace for our sisters on the journey.
- When we give grace in our conversations, we become intentional builders of others' lives, letting our words become gifts of encouragement to strengthen someone else. When we lack grace in our communication, we tend toward corrosion and the breaking down of bridges in relationships. "And never let ugly or hateful words come from your mouth, but instead let your

words become beautiful gifts that encourage others; do this by speaking words of grace to help them" (Eph. 4:29 TPT). May we *go first* to give the gift of grace and encouragement to those in our world.

- "Let us then approach God's throne of grace with confidence, so that we may receive mercy and find grace to help us in our time of need" (Heb. 4:16). I love this picture. It shows us how to run to God's throne of grace, to receive mercy and find grace, so that we actually know how to give them away. Sometimes we have to go first to the throne of God to be able to go first to give grace to one another.

- "Drive out the mocker, and out goes strife; quarrels and insults are ended. One who loves a pure heart and who speaks with grace will have the king for a friend" (Prov. 22:10–11). The Passion Translation of the same two verses says, "Say goodbye to a troublemaker and you'll say goodbye to quarrels, strife, tension, and arguments, for a troublemaker traffics in shame. The Lord loves those whose hearts are holy, and he is the friend of those whose ways are pure." When we choose to go first to give grace, we refuse to traffic in shame and we keep our hearts pure before God. We break up with drama before it comes onto the scene. Grace brings purity and truth to a relationship.

Go First to Set Boundaries and Expectations

Setting boundaries and *spoken* expectations (not just the ones you have in your head) bring health and authentic connection to any relationship.

119

Here's what Dr. Henry Cloud and Dr. John Townsend have to say about boundaries:

> Boundaries define us. They define what is me and what is not me. A boundary shows me where I end and someone else begins, leading me to a sense of ownership. Knowing what I am to own and take responsibility for gives me freedom. Taking responsibility for my life opens up many different options. Boundaries help us keep the good in and the bad out. Setting boundaries inevitably involves taking responsibility for your choices. You are the one who makes them. You are the one who must live with their consequences. And you are the one who may be keeping yourself from making the choices you could be happy with. We must own our own thoughts and clarify distorted thinking.[1]

Since we are talking about friendships of the female kind, let's quickly think about what those relationships have been like for us when they were boundaryless and rife with unspoken expectations. Don't pause for too long or you may have a panic attack. The truth is—they were a mess! Unspoken expectations bring so much strife to any relationship. I think about how Tanya and I were at a standstill with each other when we "broke up" for a season, somewhat due to unspoken expectations. I had expectations of what I thought she should do, as she did of me.

In this section, I am going to give simple starters to help you go first to create healthy boundaries and expectations in friendship. These things are not necessarily difficult to do, but it takes intentionality to apply them and put them into practice. And when you do, they bring clarity and great health.

Starter #1: Communicate. Speak your expectations. Don't assume people know how you feel or that they think the way you think. When communicating, try using lines that start with "I feel," "I think," "I would like," "I am going to," and "I am willing to." Use ownership words that show you take responsibility for your side of the fence—your thoughts, feelings, emotions, actions, and expectations.

For example, I remember going out to dinner at Vinegar Hill House in Brooklyn after an all-team meeting with our church. Tanya and I were just beginning to rebuild our friendship, and I felt afraid of hearing how I'd hurt her, but I was willing to lean in. I remember both of us speaking our expectations for what it would look like to rebuild. I said, "Tanya, *I am willing to* talk about this whenever we need to, even though *I feel* fear. *I feel* fear because I am terrified to find out how I am flawed and how I hurt you (selfish, I know). *I would like* to rebuild our friendship, and to me that looks like serious talks with the intention of reconciling things to make peace, as well as having fun together and making new memories. *I feel* excited and a bit scared all at the same time, but *I think* we can do this!"

I also had to be okay with letting Tanya communicate her feelings and expectations to me—this was not a one-way street. Our friendship is not all about me being right and having only my needs met. This brings us to starter #2.

Starter #2: Ask your friend to communicate their feelings and expectations to you. Practice active listening by not interrupting (with a comeback or excuse) and by communicating back to them what you heard them say. Don't assume you know how they feel or what they think. Verbal acknowledgment of their side of the story is powerful and has the ability to bring you to a place of repentance for how you may have hurt them, which builds a bridge for reconnection.

Safety and reciprocation are important when allowing someone to communicate their feelings and expectations. (I will talk more about becoming a safe person and attracting safe people in the next chapter.) My friendship with Tanya is a safe one, so even if she cuts me, I know I am loved, and she knows she is loved—it's a wound from a friend (Prov. 27:6). That day, we let each other know what we needed in order to see positive change in our relationship. We then acknowledged it, repented, made amends, and moved forward. Now, years later, we are flourishing in our friendship. She is my pain partner, my go-to celebratory sister, and my friend on mission. But it's taken intentionality.

In my opinion and from what I've learned, the definition of *unsafe* is when someone wants to communicate *their* feelings and expectations of you without allowing you to do the same. When it's a one-way street or when someone wants to make you their punching bag, that's often an unsafe relationship. Their motive doesn't *appear* to be love (I am not a mind reader though) but instead to be right, with no desire to reconcile, just to be heard. When you are not valued as a human being created in the image of God, it's probably time to say goodbye. You are not obligated to be anyone's doormat, especially if you have asked for forgiveness and they refuse to give it or won't relent in making you continually pay for your offenses against them (read Matt. 18:21–35).

You are a beloved daughter (and so is she), but remember, you have a responsibility to make choices and set boundaries for your life. I have found that setting healthy boundaries on your end gets you to a place where you are honest with what you want and in turn causes the other person to be honest and tell the truth as well.

Starter #3: Do what you say you're going to do.

Doing what you say you're going to do is highly effective in parenting, marriage, friendships, work relationships, dating, and so on. For example, when I'm on an airplane and I hear a parent whose child is relentlessly kicking my seat say, "Stop it or I'll take your iPad," I want to say to them, "We shall see who is in charge here . . ." *Hours* later, when they are threatening the same thing and have not followed through after I have asked the child several times graciously and with a smile on my face to stop, I *want* to turn around and say, "Liar! Follow through. Would you like me to show you how?" Obviously, that wouldn't be helpful, and I haven't done that in real life, but I realized the moment I heard them say they'll take away the iPad that they were not going to follow through because it's a thirteen-hour flight and they *need* that iPad for their sanity. Kids know when an empty threat has been put on the table, and if they're not sure, they'll test it. In our human nature, adult or child, we will test the boundaries others put in place.

If you say something like, "I won't further this conversation until I feel safe and valued" or "I won't continue to break down where our relationship went wrong in this way but am willing to hear you if the goal is reconciliation," then actually follow through and keep your boundaries in place.

The same goes for commitments we make to one another. If we say we'll check in, then we should check in. If we say we'll hang out once a week, then we should put it on the calendar and show up. If we say we'll commit to accountability in our struggles or goals, then we should check in and freely offer up where we're at instead of always expecting the other person to ask us, because we're as accountable as we choose to be. Let our yes be yes and our no be no.

Also, as much as I'd love to, and I hate that this is true, we can't force people to love us, but we can show love to others by doing what we say we will do.

Go First to Free Their Future

I remember walking through yet another season of major transition and change (because they never end—change is a constant). I was trying to navigate not only the guilt I felt for mistakes I had made in a certain relationship but also the general feeling of not being enough—which was my co-dependency issues speaking. I just couldn't do or say the right things to make peace. There was a change coming, and we both felt it. The truth is, transition is hard, even though it's a natural part of life. I mean, think of natural childbirth sans meds—who loves transition? Not one mother out there who has given birth naturally just shouted, "ME!" If you did, I applaud you. Nope, that's the part where you grab your husband's collar and say, "YOU DID THIS TO ME!" and frantically turn to the midwife and say, "I didn't mean it, I want drugs. All the drugs. These fools who speak of natural childbirth being beautiful [I am one of those fools]—I want to talk to them now and give them a piece of my *bleeeeeep* mind!" To which she says, "Too late, sweetheart, you're about to push." And your famous last words to the midwife, right before the baby is in your arms, are "DON'T CALL ME SWEETHEART!!!" Three pushes later, with the baby in your arms while you're kissing your husband, oxytocin—the love hormone—surging through your veins, you find yourself saying, "Babe, let's do this again. I love you. Isn't he perfect? Susie, you are just the most amazing midwife. I couldn't have done this without you."

Transition. It's a natural yet strange part of life, packed with conflicting emotions that don't seem to go hand in hand.

So, what happens when you're in transition in a friendship and you know it? What happens when the dynamic changes but neither of you knows what to say? It's weird, sometimes painful, and often awkward yet still needs to be maneuvered with grace, honesty, and love to the best of our ability. Some friendships don't work out, and that's hard. Some friendships just end, and there are open loops that you'll never be able to close. Some friendships simply grow apart due to distance, job changes, misunderstanding, disagreement . . . I mean, fill in the blank and make this personal. Friendships change for so many reasons. So when a friendship is in transition, what do we do? I've noticed that I tend to have a conversation in my mind, ping-ponging back and forth, trying to work out what went wrong, when instead I probably just need to pause, run to God, and ask Him what is true. And then realize that with some relationships, it's time to let go, receive His peace, and, as hard as it is, move forward. We've got to grieve the fact that some friendships just won't heal. It's also possible that in some friendships, your differences of opinion and core value systems are so incongruent that you can't seem to figure out how to do life together. And sometimes a friendship is simply unsafe, so it needs to come to a close.

To create authentic connection and fulfill your purpose with other women, you have to free some people from your life. For their benefit and yours. My husband and I have a coach who says we need to "free their future."

REFLECTION POINTS

- Even when a friendship is transitioning, if you are able to have a closing conversation, humbly ask if you've hurt them in any way and then ask for their forgiveness. They may not ask you back, but you can *go first* and ask them.

- When you set someone free from your life, refuse to stand in judgment of their life. It simply speaks to our insecurity when we have a need to diminish someone else to make ourselves feel superior. Remember, you are already justified in Christ.

- And if you need to, go ahead and unfollow them. And then choose *not* to secretly stalk them (not that I've *ever* done that)—let them go.

chapter 7

CREATING AUTHENTIC CONNECTION— IT DOESN'T JUST HAPPEN

Friendship is born at that moment when one person says to another: "What! You too? I thought I was the only one."

C. S. Lewis

When COVID-19 hit in 2020 and we began to shelter in place in New York, I don't think we thought it would last as long as it did. I mean, no one on earth really knew the path that lay before us, so one day at a time, we all just worked it out. About a month in, the monotony was really getting to each of us in our household. We all dealt differently with the grief and loss of the regular rhythms of life. Tears at awkward moments, uncalled-for anger, unnecessary levels of impatience for ridiculous things, and the desperate need to get some introvert time (with no one touching me or asking me twenty questions they can answer or google for themselves) were most often my quarantine manifestations.

One Sunday morning after we all watched Liberty online together and did discipleship after, I noticed my agitation levels beginning to rise once again, and I was irritable from my kids just being kids. I mean, hadn't we just spent time in the presence of God with biblical discussion and prayer, seemingly so holy? Yet my unholy anger was about to spew out on the citizens of the Andrew clan. I decided to call a family meeting to set boundaries and make *my* needs clear so I could stop short of cutting people's heads off for just being human around me. Boy, did the Holy Spirit lead that meeting in another direction. But here's where it started:

"Hey, guys. I just need to let you know that I need a good couple of hours alone, uninterrupted. Please just let me be alone in my room. Don't text, knock, look in the window from outside, or tell me, 'You're the only one I can ask this question to.' Unless we're calling 911, leave me alone because I don't want to explode on you all. No one has done anything wrong. I am just grieving, sad, and trying to work things through."

Paul then shared where he was at, and then our roommate Kaylee, who happened to be quarantined with us, went. Then I looked into the tender eyes of my children and thought, *How incredibly selfish it is for me to expect everyone to center their lives around my feelings and needs.* In that moment, I felt strongly that I should open up the floor to my kids to share their hurts and frustrations, along with what they needed from the family to feel loved. I said, "How are *you* feeling, and what can we all do as a family to love *you* better?" Well, my goodness. The floodgates opened up as each and every one of them vulnerably shared about where they were hurting, sad, frustrated, angry, or confused, often due to the actions of another in the room. Then they each articulately shared what they needed to feel loved. We asked for forgiveness from one another, forgave one another, and learned how to intentionally connect and give love to one another as well. It was healing, brought understanding, and created authentic connection.

Through everyone's vulnerability, tears, truth telling, and love, I was blown away at what God had done. It was powerful and honest. I couldn't believe how I had selfishly started that meeting so everyone would leave *me* alone and respect *my* boundaries, and I left more deeply connected to every person in my family. I left convicted as my children were given space to share, causing me to repent and make amends—more than once. I left *seeing* each person as powerful, in need of love, and completely unique in their God-given identity—instead of as people who push my buttons and who need to give *me* space.

In any relationship, friendships included, we have to start with our own posture when it comes to creating authentic connection. We have to lay our hearts bare before the Lord, letting Him examine our motives, all while allowing ourselves to be honest with where we're really at. We have to recognize our unmet relational needs and become aware when we're throwing them upon a new, unsuspecting friend to meet. We have to ask ourselves, *Am I in this friendship just for me, what I can get out of it, and how it makes me feel?* Even if it's unconscious, we have to let the Holy Spirit dig around in the soil of our hearts to get us to a place where there is reciprocity, mutuality, and a genuine heart to serve one another.

At the same time, don't be hard on yourself; it's going to take some time. Maybe even years. And yes, with *some* female friendships, you will have instant connection and just know that you're going to be friends for life.

Intentionality

Authentic connection isn't a fluke. It takes intentionality.

When my husband and I speak on marriage and relationships together, he often uses a well-worn illustration, and for good reason. He talks about how he schedules date nights and calendar meetings for us, and how it's not "sexy," but it builds our marriage. He asks everyone to think of an architect. "Imagine you hire an architect to put together plans to build your new house. You're not going to tell them to go ahead and 'wing it' or 'just do your best'; no, you're going to want them to have a strategy, also known as a blueprint, to build that house. The creativity and 'winging it' can come in while decorating, but the foundation, structure, and integrity of the house have to be intentionally planned so that the house doesn't fall down, even if it looks pretty."

It's the same with our friendships. What intentional measures can we put into place to love someone well?

I have one friend who has taught me so much about this. She lives on the opposite coast from me but texts or leaves a voice memo at least once a week, which may not seem like a lot, but over time it builds something. She takes advantage of the gaps in her day to make contact. It takes a minute or two of her time each week, but it opens the door for response and connection as we slowly but surely get to know each other more and more and simply get closer. It also reminds me to text her and go first too, so that I'm not always waiting for her to initiate contact in the friendship. She has become a friend I can call when things get hard or when I need wisdom from outside my immediate sphere or when I just need to be seen and heard. She's a great listener but also wise and grounded, and she gives timely advice. The thing I have to consistently remember on my end is to do the same for her, because it's not all about me and what I can get out of the relationship.

The 5 Love Languages by Gary Chapman contains tried-and-true methods to help us intentionally love one another, and I highly recommend any of the versions available, written for the different types of relationships we find ourselves in. According to his book, the five core ways we receive and give love are words of affirmation, quality time, gifts, acts of service, and physical touch.[1]

The way I receive love is through acts of service. I think that because life is so busy, the to-do list is never-ending, and the needs of those around me are so great, when you vacuum my house, do my laundry, organize a cupboard, or cook or order a meal for me, I feel so deeply loved and seen. The top two love languages of my friend Tanya are physical touch and gifts. So, the moment I see her, she gets a long heart-to-heart hug. And for her, the closer you sit to her on the couch during a movie, the better. Touch is my lowest love language, so to give it takes intentionality because it's not my natural leaning. Gifts are my second lowest, so, again, I have to think about (and don't always do the best job) getting little things here and there to let her know I'm thinking of her and that I care.

Consider asking your close circle of friends how you can love them better. And if you're like my husband, you'll have to schedule it in your project management tool or put it on your calendar to be intentional and get it done. This used to seem uncaring and cold to me, but now I understand that it's one of the greatest acts of care and love my husband gives to me—intentionality. And if you're like me, you *should* probably put it in your calendar on a regular basis because that free-spirit flow doesn't always pay off. I also find that when someone pops into my mind, it's often a Holy Spirit reminder, so simply be obedient to reach out or do what you feel led to do. The truth is, if you put it on your calendar to love me, reach out to me, spend time with me, send a meal to me . . . I feel loved, and I'm sure that when a friend is intentional with you, you do too.

Be the Kind of Friend You Want to Attract

At the beginning of chapter 6, I quoted Ralph Waldo Emerson, who said, "The only way to have a friend is to be one."[2]

My daughter, Finley, is a wonder. Not perfect, but so tender and kind. I love how she loves her friends and, honestly, how they love her. Drama tends to stay far away from her, and loyal, loving friends often surround her. If drama does come near her, she confronts it head-on, and at times that has cost her some friends. But when that happens, she is genuinely fine and relieved even.

In 2019, she tried out for the school play. She worked so hard, rehearsed her lines, sang her little heart out, and felt confident after the audition. A week later, we got the news that she didn't get the part. She was devastated. She cried, I cried, we all cried. While riding the subway home from school with her brother after finding out the news, in the middle of her disappointment, she received a text from one of her beautiful friends that lifted her out of the pit of sadness. It spoke to the truth of who Finley was, not the accomplishment or lack thereof in regard to getting a part in the school play. Finley's friend called her "intelligent, amazing, sweet, kind, beautiful, and, most of all, the best friend a girl could ask for." She admonished Finley and let her know she had her back, reminding her that she'd go far in life.

This particular friend had more wise and encouraging words to say to Finley than this blubbering mom did when her girl didn't get the part. But as I reflected on this, I realized that my girl is a magnet for these types of friendships because, honestly, she is everything her friend said in the text: "intelligent, amazing, sweet, kind, beautiful, and, most of all, the best friend I could ask for in a person." She doesn't attract gossip, she doesn't attract people who try to suck the life out of her, she doesn't attract mean people, she doesn't attract manipulators, she doesn't attract drama—because she literally doesn't have time for that, mentally or emotionally.

One evening, Tanya and I were out for dinner and a movie, and over our meal, we started to discuss some of our issues in friendship. She asked, "Why do you think you attract certain types of people? Not always but sometimes. You know, the ones I tell you to take your time with or steer clear of?" (*Nervous laugh.*)

I said, "I know we've talked about this, but I think it still trails back to unmet needs with my mom. Our relationship had some unhealthy dynamics when I was younger, and I tend to attract *some* people who need mothering or who need something from me that I wasn't designed to give them. Maybe it's because they, too, have a relational female deficit, probably from their mother, or a difficult mentor/mentee/female-pastor relationship. So, I unconsciously take on the role of an emotionally codependent mother like I did when I was a kid, and I royally screw it up every time. It never goes well and becomes dysfunctional because I always disappoint them somehow, and it's possible that the reality of friendship with me is not what they wanted anyway." That right there was revelation to me even as I said it.

So, *my* unhealed issues attract unhealed issues. *My* need to "fix it" for people attracts people who need fixing, and I always fall short. My desire to have someone meet needs in me that my mom couldn't meet is always too lofty of an unspoken expectation to put on someone else, and it tends to be the straw that breaks the camel's back in friendships. Such a mess. *But we can heal.* Go back to chapters 1 through 5 and face your woman wound, refuse to be on the outside looking in, do the work to become whole, even when it's scary. Navigate betrayal like a boss, and stop avoiding the grief that comes with it because it's not your enemy. Refuse to self-preserve because the pain of that is far worse than the potential pain you will face in any relationship. And yes, break up with drama! The drama in you and around you.

When gossip begins to surround me, or drama or manipulators or divisive people, I need to ask why. Why am I allowing it? Why am I attracting it? Yes, I need to look in the mirror and check myself, but it's not always because I'm being a dramatic, manipulating gossiper who is spreading division; sometimes it's because I'm being passive and boundaryless when I need to draw a line in the sand and say to someone, "Enough is enough!" If I want to attract something different, *I* need to change—in Christ, first and foremost. *I* need to repent of my ways, do an about-face, and begin to live differently.

Remember this as well when it comes to being the sort of friend you want to attract: Proverbs 23:7 says, "For as he thinks in his heart, so is he" (NKJV). Just replace the *he* with *she* and ponder this. If you think in your heart over and over again, *No one wants to hang out with me. I'm too much. I don't have anything to give. The shame of my situation is too much for someone else to bear,* it's probable you'll find yourself feeling lonely, reinforcing the belief that you're unlovable or too broken. It's also probable that you've set yourself up to unknowingly reject friendship when it comes knocking on your door. These are the moments when we have to fight to uncover our true identity, recognize and admit our human deficits, and voluntarily submit it all to God. Sometimes we also need to do the opposite of what we feel like doing and reach out to a friend to tell them the truth of where we're really at, cracking the door open for connection. When we do this, day by day we will begin to overflow with a new sense of purpose, wholeness, and life. We'll start to see ourselves correctly and believe we have something to give to a relationship.

Maybe you think in your heart or speak with your mouth things like "Everyone is so dramatic. What is wrong with women? Can't they just get it together? Ugh, I mean, men are so much more uncomplicated than women." If this is your way of thinking, speaking, and living, don't be surprised if you don't attract healthy female friendships. Stop and think, what do you repeat over and over in your heart? It will become your reality. What you dwell on, you dwell in. If it tends to be negative, stop your thought process in its path and ask God what is true.

I'll say this in as many ways as I possibly can: we have to do the work to become a whole person and not expect someone else to do that for us. We'll begin to attract people along the way who are doing the work too.

REFLECTION POINTS

- Take stock. What sort of friends surround you? Are these healthy or unhealthy friendships? Why do you think you're attracting the sort of friends you're attracting?
- Do a heart check with some of your friendships. Are you both only in it for what you can get? Is the

friendship selfish on your end? If yes, how can you begin to repent of your ways and serve out of love?

- Ask yourself, *Who do I need to text, call, or show up for today to love them well?* Maybe they need a thoughtful gift. Maybe it's a kind, encouraging word, some quality time, or a huge hug. Or maybe they just want some help with their laundry.

Becoming a Safe Person

Before we talk about becoming a safe person and finding safe friends, I want to talk about the safest person I know: Jesus.

Why was He so safe? Why did prostitutes, tax collectors, wealthy and poor sinners, the outcast, broken, and crippled, and your average Joe follow Him? Why did they fall at His feet or reach out for healing? Why did people trust Him? Everyone trusted Him except for the religious leaders and the people He offended, of course.

No doubt His miracles attracted crowds, but why would people chase after Him? Maybe it was to get something? I mean, we're human, right? We all have needs. But when they found Him, did He exert His power over them? Did He force them to be healed? To follow Him? No, He asked questions like "What do you need? What do you want?" not "Here's what I'm going to do, so just take it because I'm right . . . Son of God, remember?" Did He control their decisions to follow Him, serve Him, give to Him, or give their love to Him? It seems to me all of that was freely given to Him on their own accord.

Instead, He laid down his life to reconcile us back to Him. He laid everything down for the recovery of our lives from destruction so that we could have unending intimacy with Him.

He exerted self-control without the need to control others. He loves us even if we don't love Him back—He laid it all on the line and is still willing to fight for connection to us, even if we won't fight for it.

"Greater love has no one than this: to lay down one's life for one's friends" (John 15:13). Jesus is the epitome of safe: a man willing to lay down His life to bring us close, even if we choose to keep our backs turned. So, to become safe for another is to walk in the friendship with a heart to serve and to lay down our lives in order to demonstrate love.

The below Scriptures are a wonderful guide to bring change in us, as well as to know what to seek in a friend:

- **"The righteous choose their friends carefully, but the way of the wicked leads them astray"** (Prov. 12:26). Wisdom tells us to be selective, which may sound offensive because it's not inclusive. There is a time for inclusivity, but it's not when you're choosing who has access to the intimate places of your heart. That space is simply not for everyone.
- **"Whoever walks with the wise becomes wise, but the companion of fools will suffer harm"** (Prov. 13:20 ESV). Who are you walking with? And I mean genuinely walking with, and what is the fruit of that relationship? Are they bringing you wisdom, or do you find yourself in continually harmful or destructive situations?
- **"As iron sharpens iron, so one man sharpens another"** (Prov. 27:17). Sharpening one another, not stabbing one another. There is a difference between being wounded by a friend and just being wounded. Ask for discernment to know the difference.

- "A friend loves at all times, and a brother is born for adversity" (Prov. 17:17 ESV). My darkest hours and biggest mistakes have shown me who my true friends are. And I have had some pretty dark hours where "friends" left me standing alone. *But* I have a small circle of friends who have jumped down in the pit with me, loved me, held me, and ultimately wouldn't let me die there. And I believe some of my closest friends would say the same of me standing with them during their biggest mistakes and darkest hours. This world is adverse and full of pain; therefore, we greatly need one another to show up and *be* the love of God in flesh when times get tough.

- "Blessed is the one who does not *walk* in step with the wicked or *stand* in the way that sinners take or sit in the company of mockers" (Ps. 1:1). It matters who we walk, stand, and sit with. Take a moment to evaluate where you're walking and who you're going there with. Who are you standing with and what do they stand for? Is it biblical or culturally based? And who are you sitting with and what are you talking about? Sit with a mocker long enough and you'll become one.

By simply reading these five Scriptures alone, we can see that there is a biblical road map for friendship. There are safe people and not-so-safe people to befriend and unfriend. And the importance of reciprocity is key when it comes to becoming and finding a safe friend.

In his book *The Body Keeps the Score*, Bessel van der Kolk says,

Being able to feel safe with other people is probably the single most important aspect of mental health; safe connections are fundamental to meaningful and satisfying lives. . . . Social support is not the same as merely being in the presence of others. The critical issue is *reciprocity*: being truly heard and seen by the people around us, feeling that we are held in someone else's mind and heart. For our physiology to calm down, heal, and grow we need a visceral feeling of safety. No doctor can write a prescription for friendship and love: These are complex and hard-earned capacities.[3]

As I read these words, I was struck by the depth of their truth. To be able to hold space for someone and for them to hold it for you is truly one of life's greatest treasures. To be "held in someone else's mind and heart": that's what Jesus did for us, and it's also the ultimate model for safety in friendship (and any relationship for that matter).

The safest people in my life are genuine, loving, honest, and operating from a place of identity in Christ, which causes me to want to be my authentic self around them. They don't sugarcoat things, but they also don't tell the truth just to be right; they do it because they love me. We've all felt the difference between someone telling us the truth to be superior or to teach us and someone telling us the truth because they see us and want to call out the gold in us. My safe friends are not jealous when I make a new friend, nor am I when they do; they actually draw me closer to others and to God. My safe friends are also not gossips or slanderers. Beware of people who cultivate gossip and slander to share either behind closed doors with you or on social media for all the world to see. Yes, they'll do it in the name of Jesus and make it sound holy, but know this: if you join in that game, you can be sure they'll do the same to you in the future. In general, my safe friends help me become the person God has created me to be, and I do the work in my daily life to do the same for them.

REFLECTION POINTS

To attract safe people, we need to aim to be safe and powerful. So, ask yourself these questions:

- Do I know who I am in Christ, or do I look to others to fulfill my identity? It's hard to give from what you do not have or know.
- Do I speak the truth because I love my friends and want them to flourish, or do I tell the truth because I think I'm smarter or superior, or because I'm frustrated that my friend keeps making poor choices?
- Do I get jealous when my close friends make new friends and hit it off with them? Or am I happy that they are so lovable and love others well?

Healed People Heal People

Our staff and team came together via Zoom in mid-2020 to walk in healing together—we *all* needed it. It had been a rough year for the world, and our team was taking hits left, right, and center. This is nothing new in church leadership, but as a friend said of 2020 and all that ensued, "This is advanced leadership, even for experienced leaders." We decided to take a course together called Churches That Heal.[4] Healed people heal other people and create environments that can bring healing, just like hurt people actually do hurt other people. Authentic connection starts with me being connected to God, the True Vine, and then being connected to others so that we can advocate for one another to move forward and heal.

During a discussion after one of the sessions, Zinty, our Liberty Church Manzini pastor, shared these thoughts: "Sometimes when we've been hurt in other church environments, to open ourselves back up again to connection can feel vulnerable because we are opening ourselves up to the potential of being hurt again. But it's worth it." I couldn't hide my ugly-crying face on the Zoom call with our team unless I dramatically stood up and walked out. And I was sharing the screen with my husband, so to shut down our video while he was leading the chat would have also been dramatic. So, an intense, "you could make a GIF out of this" ugly cry came erupting out of me for all to see. Immediately, my friend and team member Joy texted me and simply said, "I love you." She saw the ugly cry and didn't turn away or ignore it. She went in. And after the call was over, she wrote, "Do you need a friend right now?" to which I simply replied, "Yes."

Seconds later we were on the phone together and she asked me what was going on, and I began to pour out my aching heart. I couldn't hold back the tears. Uneven breathing and tears accompanied my ugly, snotty cry. The dredged-up issues from past church hurt that I thought I had fully dealt with surprised me. They hit me like a right hook to the jaw, and I was unaware I had stepped into the ring. The left hook came milliseconds later as the most recent betrayals Paul and I had faced, right as COVID-19 hit, came spilling out of my bleeding heart and, truthfully, it hurt like hell. Also during that season, verbal assaults came at me from every direction and for various reasons in my DMs and in the comment sections on social media platforms. Logically, I know that in our day and age this has become a part of life and leadership, but when there's already a ton going on behind the scenes that only a close few know about, it just feels like being kicked when you're down—and we've all been there.

At first, Joy just listened and let me cry and talk and cry and talk some more, but then she started to break lies off of me while speaking the truth in love. She read Psalm 91 over me and prayed with authority, raining down peace in a way that felt like a weighted blanket had come from heaven to comfort me and still my aching heart. To know Joy is to deeply love her—she is a gift. In that moment (and many more that I cannot even count), she was my advocate. She brought healing to my heart that day. Why can she do that? Because she keeps doing the work in her own heart to heal. She also has advocates and lovers of *her* soul who are there to help her heal. I'll say it again: healed people heal people.

The greatest thing I can leave you with is this: you do the work in you and I'll do the work in me—because creating authentic connection doesn't happen in a vacuum.

REFLECTION POINTS

- Are you committed to doing the work to become a healed, powerful, and therefore safe person? If yes, what steps are you taking right now to walk in wholeness in certain areas of your life?
- What friends do you allow close to you? Are they doing the work in their own lives to become a powerful, healed, and safe person?
- What boundaries do you have in place when people slide into your DMs (figuratively or in reality) to teach you, hurt you, school you, make a fool of you, or "tell you the truth," when you have not allowed them access to that sort of relationship with you? What is your block/unfriend strategy (in love, of course)?

chapter 8

CIRCLES—NO, EVERYONE CANNOT AND *SHOULD NOT* BE YOUR BEST FRIEND

> Never make someone a priority when all you are to them
> is an option.
>
> Maya Angelou

June 4–10, 2010. It was our first hot and humid week of living in New York City. This was a week we would never forget.

I felt so at home the moment we arrived with my then three little people and my steady anchor of a husband, Paul, but I was also mulling over so many unknowns. Who would my friends be? Would I make any friends, or would pastoring be the lonely, friendless, self-preserving road many a woman leader had told me it would be?

When we landed at the airport, the gracious Yolande selflessly picked us up. She had no idea who we were, but was a friend of a friend (thank you, Maz) who welcomed us home with her beautiful smiling face and calming presence. She drove us to the Upper West Side, where we stayed with the amazing and hospitable Laura Michelle Kelly, who, again, had no idea who we were but opened up her home and her life to us anyway. She put a roof over our heads for what I'm sure felt like a long month with our very small (four, three, and one at the time), active children, while she worked crazy hours on Broadway. She was also a catalyst for my first and forever New York friendship with Stella Reed.

Within that first magical, frightening, wondrous roller coaster of a week in our new city, Laura suggested we meet up with the Reed family for dinner at a burger place up the street from her apartment. They had moved in May of 2009 to plant the Dream Center NYC. Listen, we were down to meet anyone we could do life with, or even just talk to, who were a few steps ahead of us. And bonus, they had kids our kids' ages!

We came around the corner to see Brad, Stella, and their two kids (at the time—each of our families now has four), Emma and Tyler. My kids were overjoyed to see other kids their size. I was overjoyed to see another crazy family who had moved their whole life in obedience to Jesus. When Stella and I said hello, it was serendipitous. We hugged that first time like we were never going to let go. We intuitively knew that we were going to need each other. Like, the harvest is plentiful, workers are few, we better link arms or we may quit and give up sort of need each other. And we weren't wrong. Stella is one of my first ports of call when it feels like the walls are closing in or the roof is going to fall on our heads or when I wonder if everyone in our church hates us. We meet somewhere in the middle of Manhattan, between Brooklyn and Harlem (our respective neighborhoods), and talk, encourage, exhort, laugh, and cry with each other. And honestly, it's usually only once or twice a year because that's what our schedules allow. And when we meet face-to-face, I realize once again that God knew what He was doing when our worlds collided. We have been through hell together. We have stretched further than we knew possible together. We have dug around the foundations of our lives and asked God to change us together. We have walked through tragedy, joy, betrayal, triumph, pain, and great celebration. God has been in it all, and to have Stella in my close circle of peers is a gift from heaven.

We need to know who gets to have our hearts and who doesn't. It's wise to be clear on our circles so that we know what a friendship is or is not. This chapter of the book could also affectionally be called the DTR (aka Defining the Relationship) chapter. We need to know where we are with the people in our lives to be able to live with healthy expectations and boundaries. And before you think that I am spouting some self-help knowledge, know that this was Jesus's model. He had circles for different reasons. Everything He did was strategic. So, before we dive into our own world and examine our friendship circles or lack thereof, let's look to Jesus.

Jesus's Circles

We can see from Scripture that Jesus operated intentionally with three, twelve, seventy-two, and then multitudes. These were His circles.

From Scripture, it seems that even Jesus knew that twelve people were nine too many to invite into every part of His life. And honestly, even the three didn't know everything about Him, only the Father and Holy Spirit knew *all* of Him. This is why Jesus would often choose solitude over connection with others: because the deepest, most vulnerable moments of His

145

life were laid bare before the Ones He was in relationship with from the dawn of time. So, before we examine the nature of Jesus's circles, let's reflect on our own lives for a moment. How often do we go to the Father, Son, and Holy Spirit with all that we are before we run to another person?

Jesus and the Three

In the most intimate, game-changing moments of Jesus's life, He had Peter, James, and John with Him, whether He was doing miracles that required unwavering faith in the room, sharing secrets of the kingdom of heaven, or in grief and heaviness.

When Jairus's daughter was raised from death to life, Jesus kicked out anyone lacking faith and exclusively brought in Peter, James, and John. If I were one of the other nine disciples, I can pretty confidently say I would've been jealous, wondering why Jesus didn't pick me to go in. But Jesus doesn't coddle any possible hurt feelings; He stays on mission and raises Jairus's daughter from the dead.

When Jesus was en route to heal Jairus's daughter, someone brought a message not to "trouble the master any longer" because Jairus's daughter had died. Scripture says,

> Jesus paid no attention to what they said, but told him, "Don't be afraid, only believe." *Then he did not let anyone else go on with him except Peter and James and his brother John.* They arrived at Jairus' house, where Jesus saw the confusion and heard all the loud crying and wailing. He went in and said to them, "Why all this confusion? Why are you crying? The child is not dead—she is only sleeping!"
>
> They started making fun of him, *so he put them all out*, took the child's father and mother and his *three disciples*, and went into the room where the child was lying. He took her by the

hand and said to her, *"Talitha, koum,"* which means, "Little girl, I tell you to get up!" (Mark 5:36–41 GNT)

Jesus brought His closest disciples and friends into a circle of trust that required a level of faith that would raise the dead. On self-reflection, I have only a very small handful of friends I could bring into a similar situation who wouldn't bring fear or negativity with them into an environment that needed extreme breakthrough.

We also see in Scripture that when Jesus's identity was proclaimed and affirmed by Father God for the second time, the first being at Jesus's baptism, it was done in an intimate setting on the Mount of Transfiguration (Matt. 17:1–3; Mark 9:2–13; Luke 9:28–36), and—you guessed it—only Peter, James, and John were there. He brought them along to pray, and He transfigured before them, His face shining like the sun (Matt. 17:2). And not only that, but Moses and Elijah appeared, representing the law and the prophets, which Jesus surpassed by virtue of His divinity, since He was the Word made flesh. This powerful and deeply intimate moment when Jesus unmasked His divinity before His close circle not only built their faith but also revealed to them the truth of who He was, the Son of God. A voice from the cloud said, "This is my Son, whom I love; with him I am well pleased. Listen to him!" (17:5).

Up until this moment, they had walked with Him for around three years, but here, He chose to reveal a part of Himself to them and asked them not to speak to anyone of the experience until after the resurrection (Matt. 17:9). Jesus peeled back the veil for them so that after His resurrection, they could attest to the truth that He was the divine Son of God. Not everyone got to see this part of Jesus while He walked the earth, just His close, trusted circle.

When Jesus ached and prayed in the garden, at His most vulnerable, before He laid down His life on the cross, He took Peter, James, and John to watch and pray with Him. They did more "sleep praying" than actual praying, while Jesus prayed in such deep anguish that "his sweat was like drops of blood falling to the ground" (Luke 22:44), but nonetheless, those were the three Jesus chose to have by His side when He was deeply distressed (Mark 14:33).

Jesus had a trusted three He brought close to do miracles with, show intimate parts of His identity to, and walk through pain and grief with. Who do you bring close to see the things of God come to pass in your life? Who do you bring close to see the kingdom of God come here on the earth as it is in heaven? Who gets to see your true, vulnerable, warts-and-all identity up close and personal whether you're successful, broken, or failing miserably? Who really knows you, like, *really* knows you? Who do you let that close? And I mean close enough to confess your sins to and open your heart, repent, and grow with through the years? And who is close to you in your pain and sorrow? Who do you trust to love you and not wound you in those dark hours? We need a close circle of trusted friends just like Jesus did.

Just because we function as a society in public spaces (i.e., social media, church communities, workplaces, etc.) does not mean that everyone gets to have or speak into every single part of our lives. I have a friend who says, "Be vulnerable with a few and authentic with many." Be careful what you share publicly and with whom, because the moment you do, whatever it is becomes open to public opinion. You have permission to allow some things to remain sacred between you, Jesus, and a small circle of trusted friends who *love* you. Like, *really* love you.

Jesus and the Twelve

Jesus did life up close and personal with the twelve apostles. He was intentional in His discipleship journey with them. Being God *and* man, He had a plan for multiplication and change that would last beyond His life on earth. Our friendships, circles, and spheres of influence and collaboration all have a ripple effect that will last beyond us, so intentionality in our relationships is simple wisdom.

> Jesus went up on a mountainside *and called to him those he wanted*, and they came to him. He appointed twelve that they might be with him and that he might send them out to preach and to have authority to drive out demons. These are the twelve he appointed: Simon (to whom he gave the name Peter), James son of Zebedee and his brother John (to them he gave the name Boanerges, which means "sons of thunder"), Andrew, Philip, Bartholomew, Matthew, Thomas, James son of Alphaeus, Thaddaeus, Simon the Zealot and Judas Iscariot, who betrayed him. (Mark 3:13–19)

"And called to him those he wanted"—does that offend the flesh or what? And it also gives *us* direction and permission. It's okay to have a circle that you *want* to have and *want* to do purposeful life with, not that you *feel like you should* have. Big difference. Because this circle of twelve represents a circle that can turn the world upside down with the gospel.

But let's also take note that the twelve Jesus picked were diverse in personality as well. Homogeneous friendship circles are not always the best friendship circles. **Thomas** was a pessimistic doubter, **Judas Iscariot** betrayed Jesus into the hands of His murderers, **Peter** was passionate and volatile—cutting off ears, proclaiming Jesus as the Christ, denying Him, and boldly leading the church after Pentecost. **James** and **John** were so intense that they were nicknamed the sons of thunder, yet John was also the self-proclaimed "one that Jesus loved" (John 13:23) and wrote more about love in the New Testament than any other author. **Philip** lacked faith to feed the five thousand hungry followers of Jesus standing before him; meanwhile, **Andrew** came through with a solution to the problem, sourcing from a boy in the crowd five small barley loaves and two fish, which Jesus used to feed all the people that day through a great miracle of multiplication (6:5–9). **Nathanael** (aka Bartholomew; see Matt. 10:2–4; Luke 6:13–16) had no deceit in him (John 1:47). **Matthew** was a tax collector, despised in Israel by his own people yet brought close to Jesus as one of His inner circle. The *other* **James** was seemingly in the background yet chosen and trained by Jesus nonetheless to further the gospel. **Simon the Zealot** was potentially an activist in his younger years, fierce with passion and zeal. I wish more of his questions to Jesus were recorded. **Thaddaeus** (aka Judas the son of James, Luke 6:16) was relatively obscure and unfortunately shared the same name as the betrayer.

The truth is, there will be messes and uncomfortable moments with the twelve in your life, like there were with the twelve in Jesus's life, but there will also be purpose, lots of good meals, laughs, life on mission, and so much more. Who are your twelve?

Jesus and the Seventy-Two

Luke 10:1–4 says,

> *After this the Lord appointed seventy-two others and sent them two by two ahead of him to every town and place where he was about to go. He told them, "The harvest is plentiful, but the workers are few. Ask the Lord of the harvest, therefore, to send out workers into his harvest field. Go! I am sending you*

out like lambs among wolves. Do not take a purse or bag or sandals; and do not greet anyone on the road.

Jesus was focused and on a mission with the seventy-two. He knew there were countless people who needed to hear and see the goodness of the gospel, and He needed workers to get it done. Therefore, His seventy-two disciples were appointed, trained, and sent to spread the gospel at a rapid rate. This was a wave of mobilization that gave momentum to the birth of the early church.

Look around your life. Who are you in gospel-centered community with? Who are the seventy-two with whom you are linking arms to share the good news of the gospel?

Jesus and the Multitudes

Then there were crowds. Countless crowds. Multitudes. "When he saw the crowds, he had compassion on them" (Matt. 9:36), and other times He walked away from the crowds, up the mountain to teach His disciples (5:1). He stepped away from the many to teach the few. Even when He withdrew from the crowds, they'd follow Him, and He would heal them all (12:15). He taught the multitudes (chap. 13) and fed them (14:19–20), and they followed Him because He performed signs and wonders (John 6:2). He escaped from the crowds to be with His Father (Luke 5:16). And ultimately, the crowd crucified Him. There is no intimacy, trust, or relationship with a crowd, so don't mistake your influence or surface relationships for something that they're not.

A crowd will praise you and follow you one moment and then crucify you the next.

What's the crowd in modern-day culture? This qualifies as social media or people surrounding you at church whom you

151

don't know but maybe know of. This is a crowd at a concert, the people in the grocery store, at the parade, walking down the street. They exist, but they are not in your immediate sphere of influence, nor do you have any sort of genuine connection to them besides existing in the same space. Sometimes they listen to you if you have the figurative mic, but you have no idea if it makes any difference, and you probably never will.

My Circles

Before I get you to intentionally think through and break down your circles, I'm going to show you how these circles are evident in my life.

I have found that crisis reveals character in us and in our *actual* friends. Anyone else? Crisis solidifies friendships and relationships because walking through pain together and healing together bring Jesus right into the middle of it all.

The reality is that my circles are a little more complex than Jesus's; although, I do have a form of what He modeled. At the center of it all is God and my family. Father God, Jesus, and the Holy Spirit get and know *all* of me. My family gets the good, bad, and ugly of me and I of them. Discipling our children is one of our greatest joys and responsibilities. Spiritual formation as a family is paramount. My husband and children are my God-given, deep inner circle. Home is my safest place on earth. My central circle is built on the foundation of Christ, with the people whom I love and who love me no matter what the season brings. Outside of that central circle are the three, the twelve, the seventy-two, the multitudes, and different circles that include close extended family, peers, and so on. Let me break this down and then give you a diagram to fill out in your own time.

My Circle of Three

These are pain partners and celebratory sisters. They are there in the mundane, through thick and thin, and they'll scale a mountain with me and walk through the valley of the shadow of death too. These women get the phone call or text when I need them to pray and go to war on my behalf for my mental, emotional, spiritual, or physical health, and they might as well move in because they are closer than sisters. These are the women I show up for too: girls' nights out, long voice memos, ER visits, actual phone calls in a world of text messages, popcorn movie nights in our comfy clothes, births, funerals, birthdays, book releases, hard days, good days, and everything in between.

There is reciprocity, vulnerability, safety, comradery, intentionality, honesty, empathy, trust, and truth in love with my three.

As I said before of Jesus, "Not everyone got to see this part of Jesus while He walked the earth, just His close, trusted circle. . . . You have permission to allow some things to remain sacred between you, Jesus, and a small circle of trusted friends who *love* you. Like, *really* love you." These relationships reflect Jesus's relationship with Peter, James, and John; a space of intimacy, purpose, *and* safety.

My Circle of Twelve

These are the people with whom I do life, train, and walk in discipleship on a regular basis. They are people who grow me, shape me, and sharpen me, and I them.

These are the people who come over for meals and break bread with our family. We laugh, pray, and grow together. We are also keenly aware that we are on mission together. Gospel purpose is at the center of these relationships.

My Circle of Seventy-Two

This circle is about mobilization. It is often our local church community, where we are experiencing discipleship in some way, spiritual formation, communion with other believers, and deployment of the gospel in practical and tangible ways in our sphere of influence.

My husband and I oversee a global family of local church communities. We equip and release the leaders of these church communities to mobilize the gospel in various spheres that Paul and I could never be in. We are also not close with everyone we are on mission with, nor will you be, and that's okay.

The Multitudes

The multitudes are everywhere we go. They encompass, for the most part, people we will never be in relationship with. Personally, in some of these spheres, I teach, lead, post on social media, and rub shoulders within literal crowds.

These can be but are not limited to people on social media, people in churches where I teach, sometimes even people in my own community of believers here in New York and beyond.

Multitudes have what I call seed-sowing opportunities. Seeds represent the Word of God, and the multitudes represent the soil of the heart, receiving or rejecting the seed. Change is often taking place among the multitudes, so how we operate within this circle is still important. It will never be an intimate circle, nor may we ever know our true impact.

Other Important Circles

Community of Believers Circle

As followers of Jesus, we need a community of believers to walk, mourn, grow, celebrate, worship, learn, pray, and commune with. A faith community is imperative, whatever shape or form it comes in. Whether you're at a church with thousands of people, a smaller community church, a house church, or something in between, this circle is vital.

As Hebrews 10:24–25 tells us, "And let us consider how we may spur one another on toward love and good deeds, *not giving up meeting together*, as some are in the habit of doing, but encouraging one another—and all the more as you see the Day approaching."

This circle can correlate with the seventy-two.

Trusted Family Circle

For me, this includes my mom, my sister, and both of my sisters-in-law. I trust them all implicitly with my life and savor the time I get with them. They're all so beautifully different and welcome to speak into my life.

You may or may not trust or be close to your family, so this circle may be an irrelevant or unsafe circle for you.

Legacy Circle

In my life, these are people who will always be there, even when we don't get to see each other all the time. They are the friends I pick up with, even when I haven't seen them for months or years. There tends to be connection without too much effort. These are low-maintenance, high-yield friends.

Peer Circle

For me, this includes other pastors and female leaders with whom I am not in an immediate faith community and usually not living in the same city either. There is separation in that aspect, and it's helpful for perspective. We are runners in the same race, on the same team, just leading in different cities and spaces, and I *need* these women in my life.

Stella, whom I mentioned above, is in this circle with a small handful of others. Similar to my three, these women get the real, honest, vulnerable me. They have an understanding (since they are also pastors/leaders) that we are all just regular humans, thrust into leadership positions in the church realm, who need safe spaces to open up, speak truth, share, break things down, and build each other up. We need people who are on the same track, running the same race, and facing the same challenges as we are, so we don't lose the plot. Comradery is the key to continuing.

Often, my meals, calls, or voice memos with these friends remind us both that we're not crazy, that we are facing the same giants, and that God is much bigger than we thought.

Neighborhood Circle

These are my pizza-eating, wine-drinking, storytelling, in-the-trenches-with-our-children friends. We meet in the schoolyard and love doing life with one another, and so do our kids.

Mentor Circle

These are the women who have been mothers in the faith to me. A couple mentors to note are Maria Durso and Lisa Bevere, who happen to be two Italian mamas who have carved out a path before me, who love and encourage me and challenge and uplift me to keep on keeping on.

Remember that some mentors mentor you from afar, meaning you're not in close, personal relationship with them. They may be people you look up to and listen to, who lead and disciple you by the way they live their lives.

Your Circles

So, now we get to apply all of the above. Take some time, days even, to prayerfully fill in the diagram on the next page. You might be blown away by the beautiful relationships you have in your life as you intentionally write them down. Others of you might find it eye-opening to see that you may have more shallow friendships than you thought you had, with not many friends who are close enough to see the intimate, vulnerable, honest parts of who you are. Still others of you may just see that there is work to be done to enable you to be on mission with others—that your friendships may have been more for pleasure than purpose—and maybe that's not a problem to solve but more of a tension to manage.

I hope this exercise opens your eyes and fills you with hope to see the people who are all around you, with you, and for you. So, let's dive in.

REFLECTION POINTS

- Don't rush this. Take time as you begin with the diagram. Reflect on Jesus's intentionality in His relationships. Refuse to feel guilty when you realize that some people in your life are closer to you than others and that some friendships aren't healthy anymore. Honest reflection is necessary here.

- Take a deep breath, pray, and maybe use a pencil, because you may need to erase and rewrite as you lean in to this exercise. It's also okay if some of these circles are irrelevant to you for various reasons. They may be built out or change over time.

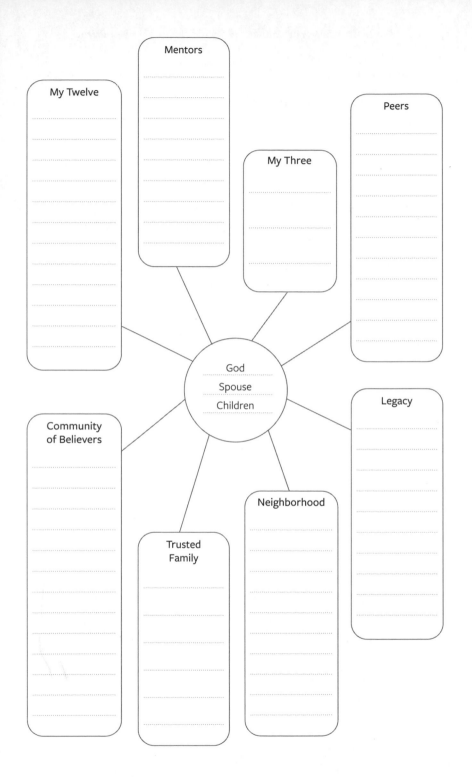

- Begin to thank God that you're not alone. Break agreements with lies that have told you no one is there for you as you begin to see the beautiful community around you, big or small.

Don't Let Fear Hold You Back

Fear of rejection is my Achilles' heel when it comes to relationships with women. What's yours? We need to know what we fear in friendship so that we can face it and overcome it.

As I sat with two friends (a married couple) to work on a project with them, I had an encounter with God that changed the trajectory of my journey—with them in particular but also in how I saw friendship. They happen to be pastors and are friends with other pastors in our world whom I have past pain with. I have faced that pain and healed from it but had an underlying fear that these two would "pick" them as their friends and not Paul and me. Yes, not a healthy way of thinking, but it had been solidified by unfortunate, weird betrayals that happen in pastoral spaces. My goodness, we all need Jesus!

We were walking through different aspects of the project when the conversation turned. My friend looked me in the eye and said, "You know, you guys are our friends *and* they are our friends. I will not pick and choose." And I lost it. I embarrassingly cried and couldn't breathe properly. Somewhere deep inside I had been waiting for them to reject me, to reject us. I had unconsciously figured they'd just stop showing up. Stop caring. Stop calling and then choose them. In an instant I realized that I had gotten good at not being chosen and had fallen into the victim trap. I think they sensed it and so, in turn, pointed out the elephant in the room. And in that moment, I was set free from a spirit of rejection.

159

I think we use the word *family* a lot, but to let people be our family—like, closer than a brother or sister—means that they get to say hard things, loving things, things that open up our hearts. It means that with them, there is a safe space to be vulnerable, to be ourselves, and not just in our greatest moments but in our weakest, most insecure, and most fearful moments too. C. S. Lewis said,

> To love at all is to be vulnerable. Love anything, and your heart will certainly be wrung and possibly be broken. If you want to make sure of keeping it intact, you must give your heart to no one, not even to an animal. Wrap it carefully round with hobbies and little luxuries; avoid all entanglements; lock it up safe in the casket or coffin of your selfishness. But in that casket—safe, dark, motionless, airless—it will change. It will not be broken; it will become unbreakable, impenetrable, ir-redeemable. To love is to be vulnerable.[1]

As adults, leaders, and human beings trying to thrive and not merely survive here on earth, we need to open up our worlds and our lives. We need to stop hashtagging #family, #friendship, or #bettertogether and instead figure out what that really looks like through the good, the bad, the ugly, the hard, the beautiful, the glorious, the uncomfortable, and the vulnerable moments of life. We need to seize fear and put it in its place. We need to wrestle with rejection and go back in for more connection, even if it's not returned. Because sometimes God sends "family" whom you get to choose, who also decide to choose you, and it's glorious. It's healing. And it's kingdom.

chapter 9

UNITY IN OUR DIVERSITY–
TOGETHER IS ACTUALLY
BETTER

Be the woman who fixes another woman's crown without telling the world it was crooked.

Unknown

The success of every woman should be the inspiration to another. We should raise each other up. Make sure you're very courageous: Be strong, be extremely kind, and above all, be humble.

Serena Williams

I remember being called out and spoken down to in front of thousands of women years ago by someone I greatly looked up to. I knew I would never be like her, teach like her, or operate like her, and honestly, I didn't want to. I had always admired and appreciated the beauty in how she expressed and manifested the heart of God. Her ability to teach and remember the Word was bar none. But when she "taught" me from the stage and made fun of me, making me feel less than, I was embarrassed, hurt, and broken. In the green room afterward, I was ignored, while the other female speakers chatted like girls in the schoolyard, sneaking a look here and there to see if I was watching them. Personally, I have sincerely forgiven her, healed, and moved on, but the idealist in me, who earnestly believes with everything I am that we can be unified in our differences, was shattered. I think *we can* have unity in our diversity as women, but unless we can appreciate, honor, and come alongside one another, we'll never get there. We'll simply be waiting for someone else to become more like us, to think like us and act like us, instead of seeing who they were made to be in the image of God.

Friendly Fire Destroys Trust

friend·ly fire

/ˈfren(d)lē ˈfī(ə)r/

noun

Military
> Weapon fire coming from one's own side, especially fire that causes accidental injury or death to one's own forces.[1]

Some of the cruelest, most agonizing moments in my life have come from friendly fire, where the person holding the figurative gun was a woman.

Since giving my life to Jesus at the age of nineteen, I've had the privilege of being in church leadership spheres where women were believed in and served alongside the men. Simply put, women had a voice and weren't torn down. I know that for many women this has not been the case. I understand that it's an incredible gift that my ability or calling has never been in question because of my gender. I married a man who advocates for me and other women not just to be at the table but to lead, make decisions, direct, teach, and come alongside. He hires the right person for the job, not the right man for the job. I have a father who has been one of my biggest cheerleaders since I can remember, and my being a woman was and is always celebrated by him. He still cries every time I preach and has been my protector and prayer warrior. In our Liberty Church culture, the women are humble, powerful, every number on the Enneagram, and every combo on Myers-Briggs and DISC. We have apostles, prophets, shepherds, teachers, and evangelists—who could all clash (and sometimes do), but I can honestly say we admire one another and cheer each other on. These women are not my competition; they are my sisters, and it is my joy to amplify their voices.

So, needless to say, I'm crushed when women come at each other, when they reduce one another to feel superior. *It simply should not be.* I do have some level of compassion when women have been taught that they don't have a place or a voice. I can understand to some extent why it's an actual fight to find your place and voice; we just have to remember that we can do this without it being at the expense of another woman. Here's what I've experienced: the kingdom of heaven looks like women advocating for one another, lifting up and amplifying the voices of one another, not competing with, tearing down, belittling, diminishing, gossiping about, judging, slandering, hating, or canceling one another. Sure, you may need boundaries with some women, but there is absolutely no need to diminish another human being made in the image of God—ever. When we come at another woman who is on our team with "friendly fire," we cause damage or death to that relationship and break trust. We can and need to do better.

Mary and Martha present a classic tale of friendly fire. Two sisters, both equally loved by Jesus, yet rivalry and judgment sit between them. As we reflect on this story, I think we can all see that Martha means well because she thinks she's right, and usually that's where friendly fire comes from—when we believe we are superior in our actions compared to someone else's.

Luke 10:38–42 tells the story of two sisters on completely different pages. Martha believes what she's doing is correct—and to be honest, I can see why, especially culturally—while Jesus says the other sister, Mary, has chosen what is better.

> As Jesus and his disciples were on their way, he came to a village where a woman named Martha opened her home to him. She had a sister called Mary, who sat at the Lord's feet listening to what he said. But Martha was distracted by all the preparations that had to be made. She came to him and asked, *"Lord, don't you care that my sister has left me to do the work by myself? Tell her to help me!"*
>
> "Martha, Martha," the Lord answered, "you are worried and upset about many things, but few things are needed—or indeed only one. Mary has chosen what is better, and it will not be taken away from her."

I completely relate to both of these sisters, depending on the day or season of my life. Martha had invited Jesus into *her* home, so of course she was preparing the meal, but the expectation would've been that the other women (i.e., her sister) would help, as that was the cultural norm. But Mary is taken into the gripping, Spirit-filled teachings of Jesus, and she is not pushed away by the Rabbi but welcomed to sit at His feet and learn. This alone is unprecedented and breaks down gender roles right in front of Jesus's male disciples. What we see here when it comes to friendly fire is a woman who is angry because she has been left alone to do all the work, while her sister lazes around listening to Jesus teach. The audacity! And honestly, if I were Martha, I would've come at my sister too because, first of all, I would've been jealous. Of course, I wouldn't want to prepare the meal either; I'd want to be sitting there taking in all that Jesus had to say. Seething anger would undoubtedly bubble up and expose my control issues in a moment like this. Second of all, I'd be confused as to why Jesus was allowing this nonsense. I mean, this sort of thing isn't allowed. This is boundary crossing! Women listening to a rabbi? Where are we, pagan Ephesus, where women have equal rights to men? Jesus, this is weird, let my sister help me. I am obviously far superior in this situation (remember, this is *my* house), so tell her to get her butt up.

So, I get Martha passive-aggressively shooting her sister down in front of Jesus and their guests. She says, "Lord, don't you care that my sister has left me to do the work by myself? Tell her to help me!" (Luke 10:40). Is anyone else cracking up? When my inner Martha comes out, everyone in the room feels it. Right after Martha shoots friendly fire in her sister's direction, Jesus brings a kind yet out-in-the-open rebuke: "'Martha, Martha,' the Lord answered, 'you are worried and upset about many things, but few things are needed—or indeed only one. Mary has chosen what is better, and it will not be taken away from her'" (10:41–42). Oh, the fire that would rise in my belly: "Don't 'Martha, Martha' me, Jesus! And don't point out my 'many things' I need to deal with in *my* home."

But the truth is, whether we subdue and/or confront our desire to take out our guns and fire on our sisters has to do with choosing the better thing—sitting at the feet of Jesus, hearing *His* voice above the jealousy, insecurity, comparison, anger, fear, and rejection that sometimes speak louder than He does.

Apparently, things get resolved after this public moment of friendly fire and Jesus's rebuke because in John 12, Mary of Bethany is back at Jesus's feet, but this time she is anointing Him with a pint of pure nard (very expensive perfume), while "Martha served" (vv. 2–3). Mary just keeps choosing to be at the feet of Jesus, but this time it seems Martha is secure in serving.

We'll stop the friendly fire when we love who we're created to be and stop expecting others to be more like us or expecting ourselves to be more like them. I sometimes wonder if Martha had a genuine hospitality gift and really loved preparing her home, making amazing meals, and taking care of everyone so that they felt loved. It's also possible that she had unspoken expectations that her sister would help in her endeavors to serve their guests. And I wonder if Mary was an empath who had always desired to learn from a rabbi and jumped at the chance to immerse herself in the teachings and the love of Jesus. Either way, it seems these sisters worked it out and allowed each other to just be who they were created to be without needing to keep calling each other out.

REFLECTION POINTS

- In a group or on your own, read through the story of Mary and Martha in Luke 10:38–42.
- In this season, who do you relate to more? Are you in a place of peace and receiving from the Lord, wondering

why the Marthas of the world can't just chill out? Or are you in Martha mode, wondering why the Marys are so lazy and can't just do what they're supposed to do?

- Are you able to take a second and choose the better thing? Are you able to sit at Jesus's feet for a hot second and ask His perspective?

One Body, Many Different Parts

When we read the Bible, we read it through a certain lens. When we show up to a church community, we see and experience it through a certain lens. When we walk into a friendship, we view that through a certain lens too. Because when we read, commune, or show up to relationships, we bring our family histories, upbringings, surroundings, belief systems, indoctrination, prejudices, fears, trust issues, unspoken expectations, and traumas. We even bring the good, life-giving experiences that we would maybe unknowingly love to replicate or, at the least, have more of in friendship. We bring ourselves to the table. That's why part 1 of this book is so important. The more self-aware we are, the more we can take ownership of our end of relationships, choosing to first put on our Jesus lens, which further enables us to turn up as whole as possible.

When it comes to unity in our diversity, why is this so hard sometimes? Why are we quick to judge, size up, and wish others were more like us?

One of my passions is helping people understand that they are a unique brushstroke in a collective masterpiece called The Church, which God is positioning, orchestrating, and building for His Son, Jesus, to return for. We are uniquely created and positioned *by Him* in every way to collectively fulfill the Great

Commission: our DNA is God-breathed, the cities and towns we live in need the reality of Jesus, our church communities are strategic and so are the neighbors we are placed near, and so on. Some of the roles and parts we play are magnificent or seen as more important than others, but only according to the world's standards (not God's). Maybe the assignment from God that's been asked of us is extremely difficult, but in the end we find that our obedience brings us satisfaction in what we put our hand to. And other times, our assignment feels hidden and meager compared to that of another person. And that's part of the problem. When we don't live surrendered to Christ and *His* daily will for our lives, we compare and contrast our calls, seasons, roles, images, family lives, relationship statuses, and so on by the world's standards, forgetting that we are *one body* with *many different* functions and parts.

I am so keenly aware that if we don't take our place with a collective obedience and deep understanding of what a great honor it is to *be* the church and *build* the church, *wherever* and *whatever* the assignment, we'll simply become critics of the bride (one another) instead of builders of her. Without honor for the collective whole of the body of Christ, we become like a bride tearing herself apart as she's trying to walk down the aisle to meet the bridegroom. What good is a torn and tattered bride screaming *at herself*, "Be more like my toe! No, be like my lung—you can't breathe without me! Don't be foolish; the hands are the best part—they do all the good work. Be like them or you'll be judged!" Does that not paint a picture of sheer crazy?! This would be a hard wedding to watch, yet *this is us*, the bride, self-mutilating and seeing our different limbs, functions, and organs as being more or less superior than others instead of coming together and appreciating the whole! We need to stop body shaming the bride and gain greater biblical understanding of how to actually have, appreciate, and walk in true unity in our diversity so that we can move the Great Commission forward.

First Corinthians 12:14–27 is paramount:

> Yes, *the body has many different parts, not just one part.* If the foot says, "I am not a part of the body because I am not a hand," that does not make it any less a part of the body. And if the ear says, "I am not part of the body because I am not an eye," would that make it any less a part of the body? If the whole body were an eye, how would you hear? Or if your whole body were an ear, how would you smell anything?
>
> But *our bodies have many parts, and God has put each part just where he wants it.* How strange a body would be if it had only one part! Yes, there are many parts, but only one body. The eye can never say to the hand, "I don't need you." The head can't say to the feet, "I don't need you."
>
> In fact, *some parts of the body that seem weakest and least important are actually the most necessary. And the parts we regard as less honorable are those we clothe with the greatest care. So we carefully protect those parts that should not be seen, while the more honorable parts do not require this special care. So God has put the body together such that extra honor and care are given to those parts that have less dignity. This makes for harmony among the members, so that all the members care for each other.* If one part suffers, all the parts suffer with it, and if one part is honored, all the parts are glad.
>
> *All of you together are Christ's body, and each of you is a part of it.* (NLT)

This whole passage is worth meditating on. I suggest breaking it down, letting it read you, and repenting where and when necessary. We have to understand that we are a mosaic, and we do not complete the full picture of God's glorious body without one another. Honestly, though, I think that's one reason why being publicly taught and corrected by a hero in the faith in front of thousands of women hurt so badly. I am simply a different image bearer with a distinct assignment and role on earth. And when I teach or impart a message to tens, hundreds, or thousands, I just don't operate as others do—I express God's heart and His Word the way He created me to. I have zero desire to be a copycat. And I truly love and appreciate the beauty and diversity in the body of Christ. One of my greatest joys as a leader in our church is giving the platform away—to trusted people, obviously. I have always felt that it's a gift in my life to midwife people's callings, open doors, and amplify other voices, which also means I've had to fight to remain secure in my unique identity and assignment and remember that raising up and releasing another sister does not diminish who I am. I get to glean, learn, and have my theology expanded as I am enlightened to others' perspectives and stories that have not been my own.

To have true unity in diversity as sisters, first we need to know who we are and embrace, love, and appreciate it, and operate comfortably in our own skin. And second, we need to begin to see, appreciate, and love who God has made our sisters to be, even if they don't think, act, look, or operate like us.

My actual elder sister, Kristin, couldn't be any more different from me. And you better believe that growing up, we clashed in every way imaginable. I used to be so frustrated that she didn't see the world the way I did. I hated that she'd never let me borrow her clothes. She said I was too irresponsible with them, and in hindsight, she wasn't wrong. I hated that she got perfect grades, was a star volleyball player, always obeyed our parents, and never drank alcohol until her twenty-first birthday—and she didn't even like it. I always figured I *should* be more like her.

I mean, wasn't she the image of moral purity and perfection? Funny thing is, I found out when we were adults and no longer entangled in cat fights or slamming doors in each other's faces that she always felt like she should have been more like me— free-spirited, throwing caution to the wind. Comparison is a killer of unity in our diversity, and so is lack of understanding and appreciation for who we are created to be in the context of who others are created to be. We need each other. Every age, stage, personality type, tribe, tongue, and expression.

Needless to say, these days my sister is one of my best friends. I trust her with my life, and her gifts of order and administration are life-giving paired with my ability to throw caution to the wind. When we come together, beautiful things happen. But that wasn't always the case, especially when we were each trying to make the other be more like us.

REFLECTION POINTS

- If the body has "many different parts, not just one part," are you aware of the part you play in the bigger picture? And if you are aware, are you honored to walk in your assignment, or do you find yourself longing to have a life like that of another sister or friend? Where has pride possibly caused you to think that the role you play is the most important one or that the church you lead or attend is the only one doing it right? Where do you need to repent and see the big picture again?
- Why do you think we naturally judge by human standards instead of God's? Reread 1 Corinthians 12:14–27 above. What stands out to you? It ends by saying, "All

of you together are Christ's body, and each of you is a part of it" (v. 27). Do you believe that to be true? In an ideal, unified, healthy, whole, Jesus-centered world, this is the aim. This is the goal—to be unified and on mission as the church, each taking our place.

- What is your biggest struggle in the comparison game? Where do you find yourself saying things like "I wish I was more like . . ." or "If only I was . . ."? What parts of you are rejecting yourself before someone else will? We, the body of Christ, need you to be you, *and* we need you to be obedient to Christ in whatever He is asking you to do! We need you to become more like Christ daily and bring others on the journey with you in becoming more like Him!

Can We Just Make Peace?

I actually *love* a good, hard, disruptive, confronting conversation if its genuine goal is to bring peace and, ultimately, reconciliation in a relationship. I am here for that. But I must say, I hate confrontation for confrontation's sake. I will go quietly into my little turtle shell if you come at me just to come at me. If it's to get things off your chest—nope. If it's to sweep things under the carpet to remove a mess from your sight so that I can carry that mess for you—nope, not here for that either. Making peace and moving toward authentic connection is messy, but it also needs to be mutual. It cannot be a one-way street. We have to remember that we belong to one another and that our faith is communal, not just individual, and, therefore, making peace is a part of the process.

The word *peace* is common in most languages. But in the Hebrew language, *shalom* is so deep and restorative. The most basic definition of the word in Hebrew means complete or whole. But what is *shalom*? Susan Perlman of Jews for Jesus says, "The ancient Hebrew concept of peace, rooted in the word 'shalom,' meant wholeness, completeness, soundness, health, safety and prosperity, carrying with it the implication of permanence."[2]

But what happens when we can't make peace with another sister, mother, daughter, female leader, coworker, or friend? What happens when wholeness, completeness, soundness, health, safety, and prosperity just won't come to a relationship, no matter our efforts, and instead all you have is brokenness, fear, lack, rejection, betrayal, and pain? Personally, one of the hardest things I find in relationships is not being able to close what I call open loops. I like things neat and tidy because selfishly it makes *me* feel better. Mess in a relationship is the worst kind of mess if you ask me, yet it forces us to the feet of Jesus, the One who is our Prince of Shalom. He is truly the only one who can bring that sort of wholeness. He is the only one who can complete us, who can bring soundness of mind and prosperity—permanently. So, when we can't make peace with one another, we must run to, cling to, and be found in the Prince of Peace.

We can't force reconciliation, even though we'd love to. But what are some steps we can take to operate powerfully in a relationship, even if they're not reciprocated?

First, ask the Holy Spirit, "What would you have me do here?" You may need to apologize, ask for forgiveness, make the first move, reach out, or be intentional. Whatever the directive is, listen to the Holy Spirit, make sure what you're hearing lines up with the Word of God, and then be obedient to do what you're being asked to do. Don't let fear of rejection stop you, even though it could be a genuine factor. As

Romans 12:18 says, "If it is possible, as far as it depends on you, live at peace with everyone." This is not an easy way to live. It requires great humility because you are not a fixer; only God can truly get in there and change things. But your act of obedience may soften the soil of one's heart.

Second, know the difference between peacekeeping and peacemaking. Peacekeeping desires to maintain peace by avoiding conflict, whereas peacemaking requires us to engage in conflict and difficult conversation while navigating a myriad of tensions to bring peace, shalom. Jesus engaged in all of the above and stated in Matthew 5:9, "Blessed are the peacemakers, for they will be called children of God." We have to be willing to wade into hard and uncomfortable things. We have to be willing to lift up the carpet and sweep out the dirt from under it to see what's been hiding *so that* we can face it and genuinely move on. When things stay under the carpet of our lives, we *know* they are there, and it causes us anxiety. Peace comes when we deal with them. I understand that there are people in our lives who may not want to engage in peacekeeping. This is disappointing because it leaves an open loop in one of our relationships. When devastation hits, with no sign of reconciliation, this is when we run once again to the Prince of Peace.

That brings me to my third point: be found in Jesus. There is just no shortcut. No magical pill. No twelve-step program to force someone into reconciliation, just the choice to run into the arms of Jesus. Only Jesus. Always Jesus. The Prince of Peace. When I am broken beyond repair because of betrayal or pain in friendship, Jesus is always my go-to. I can weep and mourn with Him. He is my safe harbor and truthful companion and the lover of my imperfect soul. He is my everything.

The Importance of Generational Crossover

I used to love sitting at the kitchen table of my grandparents' house, asking questions and just letting them talk and talk. They lived through WWI and the Great Depression and fought and served in WWII, where they met and fell in love. My grandma was a WAVE (a member of Women Accepted for Volunteer Emergency Service, a military unit in the US Navy), and my grandpa was a radioman on a destroyer, the USS *McCalla* in the South Pacific. Grandma Pat (Patricia) was his nurse in the hospital after he slipped and broke his back on the deck of his ship. They married soon after they met, like many at that time did, served their final year together at Mare Island (also where my dad did riverboat training for Vietnam), then moved to the East Coast, where they had my dad, Robert Vannaman Green Jr., in 1948.

I have great memories of my time with them at the kitchen table. All I had to do was ask one question, and they'd pull back the curtain to days gone by. It'd bring me such awe and wonder, listening to how they survived so much, and the stories were never told with a woe-is-me mentality. My jaw often dropped at the pain they'd faced; their perseverance inspired me with strength to continue on in my own life when I encountered trial, pain, or adversity. I needed their stories, wisdom, and encouragement. They are still such an inspiration to me, even though they're both now in their eternal home.

Generationally, we are better together. When we get sucked into the vortex of only one way of generational thinking, we miss out on wisdom from those who have lived a lot more life than we have or on new ideas and ways of thinking from those who are younger than us.

I can't help but think of my mentor Maria Durso—to know her is to deeply love her. If I can have one ounce of what she has at her age, I will feel like I'm killing the game. She calls and texts and laments and prays with me. She encourages me when it gets dark. She tells me stories of her struggles and exhorts me to continue. She preaches with a fire that brings me to my knees and makes me feel like Jesus may just burst through the clouds at any moment to return for His bride. And most of all, she is a mother. She nurtures and calls forth life. My goodness, we need the mothers and grandmothers in the faith to arise. Without them, we lack wisdom to bridle and steer the passion *and* pride we operate in as a younger generation. The mothers in the faith speak humble truth, and not just to be right but to correct with love when we go off course. They have the future in mind, a future that will exist without them; therefore, they need to deposit seeds of life that will bear fruit in the ages to come.

My parents helped us plant Liberty Church in 2010. I don't know what Paul and I, as two young thirtysomethings with stars (and fear) in our eyes, would've done without them. They grounded us, pastored us, held us through pain, helped raise our babies, prophesied life when all we saw was death, were mothers and fathers to countless lives, performed weddings, took people in, shouldered the burdens of pastoring, shared lived wisdom, and brought so much life to the body of Christ. If we would've dismissed them as irrelevant and too old, our church and our city would've been at a loss. They've now moved to the West Coast, as their season has changed, and their gray hair has been greatly missed. There has been a visible gap without them as we lead and shepherd a young body of believers. It only highlights to me how much we need *every* generation.

My daughter also teaches me so much. I had some fear around having a baby girl. I just didn't want to pass on the mother-daughter issues my mom and I had, which also compelled me to go after reconciliation with my mom on deeper levels. My girl, Finley, has so much of her father in her. She has a steadiness in the storm partnered with grace and grit that blow me away. She has a genuine heart to serve others and lay down her life. Watching her serve from a genuine place of pleasure challenges any selfishness in me to the core. She is tender and loving and willing to go to war for things that matter. She's an advocate for others and comfortable in her own skin. She's creative and bursting forth with ideas that always seem to be centered around bringing connection and meaning. To me, she's a marvel and so much healthier mentally and emotionally than I was at her age—which I love. She softens my edges; her tenderness causes me to repent quickly when I've hurt her. She compels me to make peace. She has made me a better woman, and we're only just getting started.

And my sister, sisters-in-law, and sister-friends. What would I do without them? They bring such beauty and richness to my life. They each release the glory of God in ways I'm not designed to and cause me to see things in a different light. Their stories, backgrounds, perspectives, and giftings remind me how much we truly need one another because, on our own, we are only one note in a song instead of a symphony of grace.

We need the daughters, sisters, mothers, and grandmothers to rise up and come together. Every voice, every age, every stage, every background, every tribe and tongue are integral to the fabric of who we are as a body. *We actually are better together and not just when we wear it on a T-shirt.* It's a lot harder to *live* this than putting it in a hashtag, saying it on social media, or shouting it from the mountaintops. It will require humility and honor. It will require time and intentionality. It will require us to lay aside our insecurities and fears to build bridges and let others step in and up where we used to be the "voice" or important one—even if it was behind a veneer of self-importance. It will require us to be secure in our own skin, own lane, and God-given assignment.

We can do this. We can do better. We can *be* better.

Imitating Christ's Humility

To operate in true unity in our diversity, we have to cling to and become more like Christ. So, let's look to the Scriptures to see just how He lived His life in relationship to humanity. Philippians 2:1–8 says,

> Therefore if you have any encouragement from being united with Christ, if any comfort from his love, if any common sharing in the Spirit, if any tenderness and compassion, then make my joy complete by *being like-minded, having the same love, being one in spirit and of one mind. Do nothing out of selfish ambition or vain conceit. Rather, in humility value others above yourselves, not looking to your own interests but each of you to the interests of the others.*
>
> In your relationships with one another, have the same mindset as Christ Jesus:
>
> > Who, being in very nature God,
> > did not consider equality with God something to be
> > used to his own advantage;
> > rather, he made himself nothing
> > by taking the very nature of a servant,
> > being made in human likeness.
> > And being found in appearance as a man,
> > he humbled himself
> > by becoming obedient to death—
> > even death on a cross!

Even Jesus didn't lord His equality with God over humanity as an advantage. He humbled Himself to step into relationship with us, and therefore, in order to follow in His way, we are encouraged to do the same with one another, to value one another above ourselves. Anyone else taking deep breaths trying to calm yourself down? This is hard. Philippians doesn't play, and neither does the book of Ephesians.

Ephesians 4:1–6 says,

> As a prisoner for the Lord, then, I urge you to live a life worthy of the calling you have received. Be completely humble and gentle; be patient, bearing with one another in love. Make every effort to keep the unity of the Spirit through the bond of peace. There is one body and one Spirit, just as you were called to one hope when you were called; one Lord, one faith, one baptism; one God and Father of all, who is over all and through all and in all.

Humility, gentleness, patience, bearing with one another in love, making every effort to keep the unity of the Spirit through the bond of peace. Friends, don't freak out and do not quit. Be kind to yourself and keep going because *living this* is going to take a lifetime of learning, growing, making mistakes, acknowledging those mistakes, repenting, changing, and moving forward.

REFLECTION POINTS

- Would you consider yourself a peacekeeper or a peacemaker? How can you move toward being a healthy peacemaker in your friendships, even if it requires conflict?

- What things have you dismissed in generations that are different from yours? Have you been annoyed that some are "stuck in their ways" or that other generations are "always on their phones"? What hurdles do you have in connecting with another generation besides your own?

- Reread Philippians 2:1–8 and Ephesians 4:1–6. What stands out to you? What in these Scriptures helps you move toward unity in our diversity in friendship? If you're going through the book in a group, share your different perspectives on these Scriptures. What do you find easy to apply and live, and what is difficult for you? Take time to really listen to one another. Acknowledge people's stories with them. Lament or celebrate with them. I encourage you to take some time and pray together too.

chapter 10

BECOMING SPIRITUAL MIDWIVES

A midwife must possess the hand of a lady, the eyes of a
hawk and the heart of a lion.

Unknown

Every woman is your sister, treat her accordingly.

Unknown

I love giving birth.

Yes, I am one of those natural-birth championing, midwife-
advocating, oxytocin-loving, "connected to my human body,
created by God to birth humans" people. I am fascinated by
the process: the pain that produces life, the travailing to bring
forth, and, in turn, the sheer joy and triumph of birth. If I
wasn't doing what I'm doing now, I'd go back to college to become a midwife. I have to admit that I do at times say the line,

"Birth is so beautiful" (obviously not while in labor), which makes *some* of my friends want to throw a shoe at me, and not in a positive way because I'm preaching so good but because they want to hit my mouth so that the talking will cease.

I'm going to say these things up front so that you don't close the book and finish reading it prematurely. If you haven't given birth to a child, this chapter is for you. If you have given birth and it wasn't with a midwife, nor was it natural childbirth without drugs, this chapter is also for you—I am not the judge and jury when it comes to birthing children. Women are ridiculously amazing at carrying, stewarding, and bringing forth life, and any way that a child comes into this world is a miracle, and it is certainly not my way or the highway. I am on #teamwomen, period. I simply grew up with a doula for a mother. Natural childbirth was all I knew and was what I was educated on, so from a young age I fell in love with and became intrigued by the body's process of bringing forth life. And I say this as tenderly as possible: if you have experienced great loss from a miscarriage or in childbirth, first of all, I grieve with you. I have walked alongside other women through this heartbreaking process, and just know, wherever you read these words in the world, I am here with you in your unimaginable pain. I pray that this chapter is healing for you in ways only the Holy Spirit can orchestrate and that your sisters come around you in deep, real, and meaningful ways.

With Women

The origin of the word *midwife* is *mid*, "together with," plus *wife*, "woman."[1] To become a spiritual midwife means that we are *together with women*, not against them. We are *for women*; they are not our competition. We are there *alongside other women* to bring forth life, not death. Friends, it is not our role on this earth to tear down, cancel, destroy, or slander another woman or to set her life on fire. The fall in the garden seems to have made us all-out enemies, but restoration and redemption here look like something tangible, not theoretical. Healing and wholeness in any relationship require action steps to be applied daily. First, we must be reconciled to God through Jesus Christ, and then we are reconciled to one another through the powerful gift of the Holy Spirit, also called *the Advocate.* We are to advocate for one another, not critique, criticize, or reject one another. This is what unity in our diversity looks like. It looks like championing and standing with one another to bring forth life.

We can never minimize the role of a midwife. Shiphrah and Puah brought life and, in turn, deliverance to the whole of Israel. The importance of standing alongside another woman while she is travailing to bring life into the world cannot be diminished. If Shiphrah and Puah wouldn't have understood their role as midwives in the times in which they were living, they would've brought death and destruction to an entire people. Instead, they delivered the great deliverer Moses.

Now that sounds amazing—"delivering the great deliverer"— but let's be honest, standing with other women in times of oppression, heartache, fear, discomfort, and pain is not easy. It takes us dying to ourselves to lift, help, and come alongside even if doing so puts our lives in harm's way. The time surrounding Moses's birth was devastating for the people of Israel. They were God's chosen people, but they were greatly oppressed by Pharaoh in Egypt. Pharaoh saw God's people growing in strength and number, and out of fear, he said, "Come, we must deal shrewdly with them or they will become even more numerous and, if war breaks out, will join our enemies, fight against us and leave the country" (Exod. 1:10). He oppressed them with harsh forced labor to build the cities of Pithom and Rameses. Israel became enslaved to Egypt, but God continued to multiply His people despite their oppression. Because Pharaoh couldn't stand in the way of, nor stop, the living God, as a last-ditch effort, he instated a genocide of all males born to Hebrew women and asked the midwives to execute his demonic plan. But it's not in a midwife's DNA to bring death.

> The king of Egypt said to the Hebrew midwives, whose names were Shiphrah and Puah, "When you are helping the Hebrew women during childbirth on the delivery stool, if you see that the baby is a boy, kill him; but if it is a girl, let her live." *The midwives, however, feared God and did not do what the king of Egypt had told them to do*; they let the boys live. Then the king of Egypt summoned the midwives and asked them, "Why have you done this? Why have you let the boys live?"
>
> The midwives answered Pharaoh, "Hebrew women are not like Egyptian women; they are vigorous and give birth before the midwives arrive."
>
> So God was kind to the midwives and the people increased and became even more numerous. And because the midwives feared God, he gave them families of their own. (Exod. 1:15–21)

These midwives protected life (that of each woman giving birth and of her child) because they feared God and *not* man. When we become too accustomed to the ways of this world, we stop protecting life—spiritually and physically. We stop protecting one another. We look out for ourselves and forget that we belong to one another. Shiphrah and Puah risked everything for the Hebrew women, and because they did, Moses was born, rescued, and brought up as a prince in Egypt, garnering the authority to one day speak before Pharaoh and cry out, "Let my people go!"

Relationship above Rivalry

I remember being minutes away from pushing to bring our second son, Jesse Freedom, into the world. I had chosen to do most of my laboring at home with my mom and Paul. Right before we left for the hospital, my mom caught me sitting on the toilet (because it was just so comfortable), shaking uncontrollably in the middle of transition, and she said, "What are you doing in here!? We have to get to the hospital ASAP unless you want to have this baby in the toilet. You are about to give birth!"

Luckily, the hospital was across the street from our townhouse in Sydney, Australia, at the time. We drove—yes, drove—across the street because gravity would've birthed my son on the sidewalk (*footpath*, for my Aussies). We walked into reception at two a.m., and it was dead quiet. The receptionist took one look at me and said, "Get her upstairs unless she wants to have that baby here on the floor. It happened last week with another woman, and I don't want it to happen again."

We got up to the birthing room, and one of my midwives from my remarkable team of seven (yes, seven—Australia knows how to do natural childbirth), whom I had gotten to know over the gestation period, was there to greet us. Our friend Sarah, another midwife and friend from church, got there right on time too. We wanted her to be a part of the birth with us as well. I got undressed, put on my gown, got up on the bed, and waited for my midwife to check me to see how far I was dilated. Instead of checking me, she quietly milled around the room, full of peace, preparing everything that was needed to welcome Jesse Freedom into the world. The atmosphere was calm as I breathed through back-to-back contractions.

At one point, I started to get frustrated and abruptly asked, "Aren't you going to check to see how dilated I am?" I mean, I wanted to know if I still had hours of labor to go or not. She simply smiled at me and said, "Actually, I'm just waiting for you to push. I can tell that you're ready, but I can check if you'd like me to." To satiate my desire for information (also, I'm a rule follower, so I wouldn't push if I wasn't allowed to), she checked me and simply said, "Yup, ten centimeters. You're good to push when you're ready."

As my people gathered around me, Sarah and my midwife stood watching and let me know when to push, when to breathe, and when to hold and not push, knowing the inner workings of the body and its divine capabilities. My mom watched over me and silently prayed, advocating for me when needed. And my husband, Paul, was being coached on how to deliver Jesse— gloves on, ready to catch his second son. Three pushes later, we had a beautiful, nine-pound, screaming baby boy, all plush and pink, with a headful of dark-brown hair. We all laughed as he literally burst forth into the world, ready to let everyone know he was here.

The relationship I built with my midwives over a forty-week gestational period was integral to having a trusted space in which to give birth in such a safe and peaceful way. It would've been weird if my midwives were in some sort of rivalry with me, making sure I knew that they knew more about labor and delivery than I did. No, they got to know me, my desires, my fears, my hopes, my level of health, my experience in childbirth, and then they came alongside me to see the dream of life realized.

Midwives watch over, believe in, and remind mothers what they're created to do. They try not to interfere with the natural process, understanding that pain brings forth life. Midwives don't dull the pain with medicine unless it is necessary for relief, in the birthing plan, or asked for by the one giving birth. Even then, options for what is available are always discussed to empower the woman in labor for the journey ahead. When problems arise that put the mother and child in danger, midwives do not give in to fear but are trained to problem solve and do everything humanly possible to bring life into the world. But if tragedy strikes and death prematurely comes, they are not dismissive of the pain that ensues for the mother who is in the pit of devastating despair. They give space to mourn and grieve the loss of life but stand alongside—*with women*, not against them.

And this is the call to *becoming spiritual midwives*. When our sisters and friends are pregnant with a dream, may we be women who understand their created purpose and stand alongside them to bring that dream into reality. When they travail in pain to see that dream realized, may we be the sort of friend who stands by them, holds their hand, and gives them their options in the midst of pain and who also reminds them that facing pain brings life and freedom. When our sisters or friends are in danger, may we be women who don't give in to fear but train and arm ourselves for battle in worship, prayer, and problem-solving in the spiritual realm, bringing heaven to earth, because we were given the keys of the kingdom (Matt. 16:19). And when the worst comes to our sisters' and friends' lives—death, destruction, and earth-shattering pain—may we be women who don't walk away but come alongside and weep with those who weep, mourn with those who mourn, and hold one another when the season calls for it so that we can move forward—together. That's what a spiritual midwife would do. But here's what we have to understand:

relationship—creating authentic connection—is integral to walking this out.

The Midwives Alliance North America (MANA) *Position Statement* says,

> Throughout recorded history, women have assisted other women in giving birth. *Midwives enter into a relationship of equality with women* that constitutes the foundation of midwifery care and contributes significantly to the safety of homebirth, low rates of intervention, and satisfaction with the experience. *Because the relationship is the cornerstone of quality care, homebirth midwives spend generous amounts of time with women to foster familiarity, comfort, and mutual trust. Through open communication, deep listening, and respect for the woman's culture, self-knowledge, intuition, and values, the midwife honors each woman's journey.*[2]

All women are created equal, no matter what you have been taught, what you have experienced, or what you believe because of what you've seen. Every woman deserves dignity, no matter how broken, lost, in pain, or marginalized she is—we are all created in the image of God. But we must understand this: genuine connection, or relationship, is what builds quality of care for one another. This is how we hold one another. It cannot be done in isolation; it has to be *lived*. We have to actually be together to share stories and build trust, which fosters empathy and compassion, enabling us to help one another bring life to the planet and not death. When we "foster familiarity, comfort, and mutual trust" and practice "open communication, deep listening, and respect for the woman's culture, self-knowledge, intuition, and values," we begin to genuinely see each other and the beautiful part that each of us plays as uniquely created women in God's divine image.

Becoming Spiritual Midwives

So that we don't simply hold this as an ideal but live it out in our daily lives, let's look at what it means to become a spiritual midwife as we reflect on how a midwife operates. These are all things I observed and remember from my personal experience birthing my four children, all with midwives. The first three were born in Australia with a team of midwives, and the fourth was a home birth in Brooklyn with two midwives.

Midwives Celebrate Women, They Don't Diminish Them

When I moved to New York and was pregnant with Sam, I did a few hospital tours to see what their midwifery programs were like. Now, I am a feeler, so the atmosphere of the hospitals we visited left a deep impression on me because I tend to pick up on everyone's stuff, like an antenna searching for a radio station. This can be great from a place of empathy, but other times, it's just overwhelming. At the hospitals we toured, I remember the looks I got from some of the staff. One in particular, at reception, did a slight eye roll at the sight of a group of pregnant women and their spouses walking through. Like, "Here come these rookie idiots with their birth plans." When some of the women had vulnerable questions, they were belittled and talked down to. I wanted to fly off into a rage, as this wasn't my first rodeo (fourth human), and I desired to soothe the fears of the mothers and fathers asking their questions. No need to make them feel like fools and diminish their valid concerns. Few things get me angrier. Needless to say, I found a midwife in my neighborhood who lived up the street from me and did home births. For wisdom's sake, we mapped out the nearest emergency room and EMT dispatch just in case. I needed to find someone who celebrated me as a powerful woman made to give birth and who didn't diminish my cares, concerns, or questions.

We *do not* become more powerful when we diminish others' lives, questions, fears, concerns, or experiences just because they're not our own. We gain nothing. We become women pitted against each other. To become a spiritual midwife, we have to get good at celebrating the journey and life of another person, even if we can't necessarily understand it. The truth is, they're living *their* life; we should live ours and stop considering ways they could be more like us.

Imagine if my midwife was like, "Well, your feelings, questions, and journey are invalid because I haven't walked through that before." No, all my midwives (whether they had given birth or not) were overjoyed at being a part of my journey, jumped in alongside me, and celebrated every milestone. They celebrated me and the life within me. Remember, the word *midwife* means "together with women." When we are truly together, we can't help but celebrate one another.

Often, we criticize and belittle other women when we see them as a threat to our position, place, or way of thinking and living. Women are not your competition (except when they are because you've let them be), so if this is a core problem for you, I'd suggest asking yourself why. Why is it that when others get or already have what you want, do what you want to do, or simply do what you deem is the wrong choice for them, according to the gospel of (insert your name), criticizing how they're living their life becomes as natural as breathing? Criticizing *our* identity is what Satan is in the business of doing, so let's not help him out with our sisters. We're on the same team, so pick the right side.

Midwives Stand with Women, Not against Them

Remember Shiphrah and Puah? They had the backs of the Hebrew women. They didn't allow fear of man or their reputation to stop them from doing what was right in protecting the sanctity of life. It's our job to have each other's backs, cheer each other on, and midwife the dreams within one another's hearts.

I remember when I was twenty years old and newly saved, all I wanted to do was move to Australia. I couldn't tell you why the pull was so strong, except that the Holy Spirit was drawing me, and in hindsight I see that God had the next ten years of my life mapped out there. At the time, I was working as a barista, a baker (those are some early-hours people), and a teacher at a daycare. I was trying to save as much money as possible, but it was coming in like the slow drip of an IV, even though I was hustling and working my tail off.

My pastor at the time wanted me to take a trip to Australia before I made the final decision to move my entire twenty-year-old life there. I was devastated because I wasn't making enough money to throw thousands of dollars at a trip to just visit when I was trying to save thousands of dollars to *move* there. Little did I know that behind the scenes, my big sister, Kristin (who, remember, used to be my rival but had become my best friend), was raising money for me to go on the trip. One night she came over and presented me with a letter she had written to a certain group of people in my world at that time, telling them about my dream and her desire to get me there. I'm crying remembering this moment as I write because it was so selfless and kind. The look of joy on her face to stand with me in my dream, well, I'll never forget it. She handed me checks and wads of cash that people had given to her to give to me. She didn't just say she believed in my dream; she helped fund the dream trip to see if Australia was my new home. And sure enough, it was.

The trajectory of my life would be vastly different today if my sister hadn't done that. Who knows where I'd be if I would've lost hope and just stayed in Spokane. I wouldn't have met Paul, I wouldn't have my four beautiful kids, and we wouldn't have moved to New York City, where I now sit writing this book. And my sister was a catalyst who stood *beside me* and *for me* and not in my way. In becoming a spiritual midwife, whose dream can you help fuel, come alongside, or get out of the way of?

Midwives Advocate for Women Instead of Harming or Mistreating Them

One of the most beautiful things midwives do is advocate for women. They believe in the power of women. And an educated woman who knows what her body is capable of and knows her choices in birth, well, she's unstoppable.

Advocate means "a person who publicly supports or recommends a particular cause or policy" (noun) and "publicly recommend or support" (verb).[3] I love that a name for the Holy Spirit is "the Advocate." John 14:26 says, "But the Advocate, the Holy Spirit, whom the Father will send in my name, will teach you all things and will remind you of everything I have said to you." I always get this picture of Jesus sitting at the right hand of the Father, interceding for us (Rom. 8:34), while the Holy Spirit is intimately involved in that intercession and is also moving on our behalf. He's advocating for us, going back and forth between the Father, the Son, and us, reminding us of what we have learned and read so that we are empowered to move forward.

For us to advocate and become spiritual midwives for one another, we have to be in the business of reminding our friends of the truth. We have to remind them of who they really are. We have to remind them of what they've learned, what they're fiercely capable of, and the power and potency of the God dreams in their hearts, and we have to support them with a fire in our own hearts until they get there! Advocating for other women is such a powerful choice. It removes our insecurity as we lift up, open doors for, share the mic with, and cheer on our sisters!

Midwives Seek Understanding and Don't Rush to Judgment

I have always been afraid to ask a stupid question. Even though some say, "There are no stupid questions," I beg to differ. I was scarred for life in algebra when, after I asked a question, the teacher said, "Would you like to sign the dumb rock?" You better believe I never asked a question in that class again, let alone in any math class. And honestly, I stopped asking questions for a long time in most learning situations, or anywhere I felt inferior or inadequate or feared being made the fool. That particular math teacher didn't seek to understand my question or what I needed to learn to move forward. No, he shot me down, embarrassed me, and silenced me for a season. Good thing I've grown up, but at times, I still have to overcome and rise up when I feel misunderstood or inferior. Anyone with me?

This is why I love midwives. To them, no question is a dumb question. They seek to understand, come alongside, hear you out, and listen to your concerns, your fears, or your lack of understanding to help you learn and grow so that you can be prepared for all that lies ahead.

To become a spiritual midwife is to seek some understanding in regard to your sisters' and friends' journeys and all their questions. You may not share in their experiences or concerns, but you can still come alongside to understand them and even be a source of information if you're invited into that space of discovery.

Midwives Encourage Vulnerability—There Is No Room for Shame in the Birthing Room

I remember speaking at a certain church where a woman in front of me began travailing in prayer. The only way I can describe it is that it was like she was in labor. The sounds were the same primal sounds. I felt the Holy Spirit draw me to come alongside her. As I touched her shoulder to pray with and support her, she grabbed my hand and drew me closer to her. She was laboring to bring something forth in the spiritual realm, and I was invited into a very intimate and vulnerable moment in her life. I wrapped my arms around her, and we began to hum and rock in unison. I don't remember how long it was, but there were tears, and a deep knowing that God was bringing heaven to earth. Toward the end of our time together, sheer joy and praise to God came out of both of our lips. We hugged for a long time and chatted only for a moment, because no words were needed to describe the shared experience we'd just had. The vulnerable space was known between us. Now, people looking on could have been like, "Well, that's weird. Why are they doing that?" but there's no room for shame when God desires to do something beyond what our physical minds can comprehend.

Giving birth is vulnerable. With our first child, I remember being so uncomfortable in any of my "birth clothes." Yes, I had planned an outfit to birth in so that my pictures after the fact would be cute. Little did I know . . . Anything that was touching my body (humans included—do *not* massage me) was irritating, so I ripped everything off. It was not in the birth plan to be naked as a jaybird. Now, strangely, it wasn't like that for all my children, but this particular time, being proper was the last thing on my mind. Whatever it took to get this kid out, that became the birth plan.

Imagine if my midwives had slung shame into that moment: "Um, we're uncomfortable seeing you naked. Can you please put your clothes back on? Also, we're just going to catch the baby with our eyes closed and not look at your, um, well, you know. We can't say the v-word. That's embarrassing." The antithesis to vulnerability is shame. When we operate from that place in our female relationships, we shut down our ability to genuinely connect with one another and we stick fear right in the middle of the relationship. The moment *we're* willing to be vulnerable, we open the door to encourage another sister to do the same.

When There Is Danger, Midwives Have a Plan to Bring Forth Life

After two and a half hours of pushing, Zeke, my firstborn, came into the world. He was finally placed on my chest, only to be swiftly ripped back off me. He wasn't breathing. The feeling of sheer joy and then total shock that he was taken from me after all that work hit me hard.

But no one freaked out, so, therefore, I wasn't afraid; nor was Paul. My mom, on the other hand, knew exactly what was going on and began to fiercely pray in the Spirit. She told me later that when she saw him, under her breath with forceful authority, she said, "Not this baby!" and then went into intercession. The response of the midwives, doctors, and nurses that flooded the room, along with that of my mother/ doula, brought an atmosphere of faith, not fear. They had a plan. Zeke was resuscitated and sent to the NICU for only two hours (it was supposed to be twenty-four), where he miraculously recovered. He showed signs of hunger, and before they could give him a bottle, I requested to nurse him instead. They brought him in, and I locked eyes with my little guy for the first time, tearing up at his intense stare (that he still has). Overjoyed, I fed him, as he attached like a champ, and we bonded just hours after our shared trauma in the delivery room.

After the fact, one of the midwives in the room told me that there was genuine danger that day of losing Zeke, but they had a plan to bring life. When our sister is in danger, spiritually or physically, do we have the guts, grit, and determination to stand with unyielding strength, even when she can't? When an actual spirit of death hovers over a friend's life, what do we do? We need to have a plan to fight and bring forth life when death knocks at a sister's door. Intercession and prayer are powerful weapons. Also, showing up is a powerful weapon so that they know they're not alone in this fight. Listen, I'm not talking about codependence; I'm talking about being the peaceful warrior who comes alongside, jumps in the pit, is unafraid of the cold, hard facts, and doesn't give up. We all need that person in our lives, and to one or a few, we need to be that person.

Midwives Don't Ignore Grief but Create Space for Lament

When the worst possible scenario happens and a beautiful baby is stillborn, midwives don't move on; they create space and help to guide a journey of grief and lament for the parents. They have protocols and appropriate ways to respond and support. They approach conversations in a sympathetic, empathetic manner with respect and regard for the parents and the stillborn infant: referring to the child by name, facilitating space for the parents to engage in communication about all that has taken place. Midwives enable the parents with different yet specific choices in their time of grief, like allowing time with their newborn, or not if they aren't ready or willing. Other options are presented, like skin-to-skin contact, taking pictures, and making memories, all to aid in the grieving process. They work with their staff and team (other nurses and doctors) to shelter and protect the parents to ensure nonduplication of difficult tasks that are involved in the loss of a child.

When our friends face the worst, how do we respond? In becoming spiritual midwives, we can't rob others of the grieving process because we feel uncomfortable or don't know what to say or do. How can we become sisters who create and share space, even if we have nothing to say? Sometimes the ministry of presence is powerful enough. It's important that we provide specific options or ways that we can serve, like grocery shopping, bringing over meals, taking care of their kids, cleaning their house, paying the rent, or sending them off for a free mani-pedi so that we can intentionally love our friends in their process. Providing specific options ensures that they don't have to make any more difficult decisions than they already have to in a time of loss or grief.

How do we increase our empathy, our ability to understand and share the feelings of another person? Maybe we can't relate to their situation because it's never happened to us, but we *can* jump into the dark and devastating moments of their life and walk with them. To further the birth analogy, we may have never given birth, but we can still be in the room with a sister in the midst of her pain.

Midwives Are Generous with Their Lives

Midwives are always on call. It is not glamorous, but it is generous. To lay down your life, calendar, and comfort for another is generous. Midwives are there to serve, make a way, and empower. They don't always get thanked for their time, and many people don't understand or appreciate their sacrifice, but they do it anyway, for the love of the calling.

What about us? As spiritual midwives, are we generous with our time? With our influence to lift up, amplify, and open a door for another? Are we generous with our hearts when we need to be? What about our treasure? And are we generous even if there is no honor and no one says thank you? Pastoring and church planting are often thankless jobs, so it's a good thing I'm not in them for the praise. Just check my inbox: there are more issues, criticisms, and "this is why I'm leaving" or "what you can do better" letters than thank-you letters. I do this for God, and I do it because I genuinely love people and believe in the beauty and power of the church. I do this because I want to see every knee bow and every tongue confess that Jesus Christ is Lord forever and ever, amen. I do it because people need the reality of Jesus, not just an idea of who He is, which means it takes a conscious effort to be generous and "on call," no matter how I feel.

I am also passionate about using my influence (whatever or wherever that may be) to open doors for other women in my life, which has occasionally been brought into question by other pastors or leaders. Some of them have reached out to me to ask if I was okay with what other powerful women on my team were doing, launching, leading, creating, writing, and so on, which felt like an alien question. These women are not my competition. We are in healthy, reciprocal relationships with one another, so there is no need for rivalry.

Midwives Empower Women to Do What They're Created to Do

At the end of the day, midwives empower women in their God-given, created ability to bring life into the world. You, friends, are created to birth life—spiritually and physically.

MANA's *Position Statement* says, *"Birth works best when a woman is inspired to be confident in her abilities, well informed about her choices, and supported and affirmed throughout labor. A significant transformative experience for women, babies, and families, birth is best supported when it takes place in quiet, undisturbed surroundings. Midwives have reverence for the individual woman, are responsive to the complex factors that affect pregnancy and the unique unfolding of labor, and are patient and attentive to each woman during birth."*[4]

May we be women who cause other women to walk confidently in their unique, God-given abilities. May we create spaces where women are informed and affirmed. May we create environments where peace resides and life comes forth. May we be patient with and attentive to each of our sisters and their distinctive stories and assignments here on earth, releasing them to be all they were made to be in Christ. And may we empower, encourage, and strengthen our sisters to run their race with endurance that lasts until His kingdom fully comes here on earth as it is in heaven.

REFLECTION POINTS

- What stood out to you in the story of Shiphrah and Puah, and why? How can we be people who deliver great deliverers?
- What aspects of becoming a spiritual midwife seem like huge hurdles to you? What can you do or ask a friend to do to help you clear those hurdles in order to love and believe in others in a more genuine, vulnerable manner?
- What part of being a spiritual midwife resonates with you and comes easily? Why?
- Take a moment as we bring this book to a close (don't miss my final letter, though; we're not done just yet) to admonish, encourage, and lift up another sister in your world. What is the Holy Spirit leading you to do? Do you need to call her? Show up at her house and love her? Send her flowers? Write an email to remind her who she is and what she is called to do? Plan intentional time to meet weekly or monthly? Do you have a God assignment together that you've been delaying and, after reading this, realize *now* is the time to begin? Do you need to plan a girls' day out to make her feel like a million bucks? Whatever it is, before you close this book (after you read my final letter, of course), text, call, show up, put it in your calendar, make it happen! Let's live this out—*together*!

final letter

Friend,

Take a deep breath. Maybe two or three.

We did it. We faced some stuff together. In ourselves and with our friends. We held grief and hope in tension at times, didn't we? It was grueling and ugly in certain moments, wasn't it? Painful and powerful all in the same breath, right? I mean, at least it was for me as I wrote these words. Writing this book tested everything I believed about friendship and made me sure of what was true. God always takes me deeper when I write, and He won't allow me to put pen to paper (or fingers to keyboard) with anything that is less-than-lived wisdom. No head knowledge allowed on these here pages.

I want to encourage you: keep going. Keep facing yourself, digging deep, and breaking up with the drama that you find yourself in or that you've created. Be militant about walking in wholeness with Christ, no matter the cost. And keep going *first* to create authentic connection, even when you wish someone else would.

Don't worry, sometimes it just won't work out. Things will fall apart and you'll miss the mark, but don't allow failure to cause you to isolate and give up on female friendship altogether. Go ahead, powerfully define your circles and don't apologize for it. Keep the circle of those who are close to you in intimate and vulnerable spaces small. You don't owe anyone an explanation for that.

And for goodness' sake, let's remember that together *is* actually better. Let's stop wearing it on a T-shirt if we're unwilling to do the work, build bridges, and walk it out. Look around you. The unique beauty that God has put in every single woman needs to be drawn out, encouraged, and championed. We are sisters—period. And you may be just the person to open a door for someone else's dream to come true. Be that spiritual midwife you wish someone would've been for you, because we can't afford to stand back and settle for shallow connection if we're going to fulfill our purpose within the Great Commission together. We are meant to be *together with* women, not against them.

The truth is, walking in genuine friendship has been (and still can be—even after writing this book) one of the biggest hurdles and fears I personally face. But I refuse to give that fear the power to define my relationships now or in the future. Because some friendships have also been an overflowing fountain of joy throughout my entire life, and I truly believe that there are bigger plans at hand here than just having a good circle of friends. Destiny and purpose that bring heaven to earth are woven into God-breathed friendship.

As we turn the final pages of our journey together, I can't help but think of Mary and Elizabeth—what a picture of purpose in friendship (read Luke 1). Two women who said yes to God and carried the destiny, hope, and salvation of the nations in their respective wombs. Mary carried Jesus, and Elizabeth carried John the Baptist, who would prepare the hearts of the people to make way for the Savior of the world. They met with each other, pregnant with purpose that shifted the destiny of the world, and when Elizabeth heard Mary's greeting, Scripture says that "the baby leaped in her womb, and Elizabeth was filled with the Holy Spirit" (v. 41). She had an innate knowing right away, by the power of the Holy Spirit coming upon her, that Mary was carrying *her* Lord and Savior. She said, "But why am I so favored, that the mother of *my Lord* should come to me? As soon as the sound of your greeting reached my ears, the baby in my womb leaped for joy" (vv. 43–44).

Oh, friend, may we be a company of women who are so pregnant with purpose that when we greet one another, we shout for joy at the destiny we are each carrying within us to see God's promises fulfilled—*together*. May our God-breathed dreams leap in our respective spiritual wombs, causing us to rise up with courage to bring forth life and heavenly strategies here on earth.

Just remember that good things take time, and genuine change takes intention—so don't be hard on yourself. Simply take it one day at a time. In the years to come, you'll look back in the rearview mirror of your life and be amazed at what God has done as you've partnered with Him to uncomplicate your friendships, avoid and break up with drama, create authentic connection, and fulfill your purpose—together—with other unique and powerful women. Don't give up.

All my love,
Andi

acknowledgments

Mom—thank you for tirelessly loving me when I rejected you and pushed you away in my pain. Thank you for praying and believing that things could change and be restored for us, even when hope seemed lost. Thank you for owning your mess, asking for forgiveness, and always loving me for me. You have truly taught me what it is to fight for a relationship. You have shown me how to forgive when things can't be reconciled with someone, and you have taught me how to release what is not mine to fix or carry. I love you more than I could ever say, and I honor you.

Kristin—I am so grateful to have a big sister like you. I've learned from years of doing life together that our differences are beautiful. For years we couldn't get it together, but once we did, purpose and destiny became the fruit of our sister-friendship, and it is so powerful. You never gave up on the mess that was me, which led me back to the Lord in college. You helped catapult my life toward Australia and, in turn, my husband. You're a constant support at She Is Free each year, in my hotel room with me, behind the scenes, praying and loving me like no other when I'm nervous, and my goodness, so much more. I love being your sister. You are a gift to my life.

Finley—sweet girl, you have taught me more than you will ever know. The moment you were born and peacefully looked into my soul with your tender eyes—I was a changed woman. My heart softened, and a longing arose within me to be a better mom, woman, and example for you. I love how you fearlessly walk in your identity, intuitively walk in integrity, deeply love like Jesus, and are servant-hearted in the purest of ways. I also love how you challenge me and call me on the carpet when the moment calls for it. You are a sign and a wonder, and it is an absolute honor to be your mother.

Brittani—my childhood best friend—what memories we made: from playing "olden days" in the backyard and Barbies in your huge Barbie house (I was always a tad jealous of that Barbie house), roller-skating in the basement to Rick Astley and Amy Grant, eating snacks while watching *Anne of Green Gables* every Sunday on PBS, having sleepovers, playing softball together from age five to nineteen, cheerleading, and going to Disneyland with our moms to walking through the heartbreaking cancer journey with your mom, who was like my second mom. Funerals, weddings, tragedy, and triumph—you taught me more in friendship than you'll ever know. Your relationship was a steady anchor in my childhood and teenage years, and your consistent love shaped me. Thank you for being such a beautiful friend. I only wish we lived closer together!

Tanya—I thank God every day that we found each other at that barbecue party back in the summer of 2000. Our love for '80s music brought us together, and it has been a destiny friendship ever since. Thank you for being a friend in and through every season. You knew me before I was ever in ministry, and you don't need anything *from me* in ministry except genuine friendship in return. It's rare to find someone who knows you—like, really knows you, warts and all—and still stands by your side. I can't thank you enough. Know this: I will stand by you all the days of my life. Love you, friend.

Camille and Jessi—I won the sister-in-law lottery big-time. Both of my brothers chose *extremely well* in the wife department, and I gained two true friends. Each of you in your own way has been an unshakable sister and friend. You have both been safe harbors in and through various seasons of my life, and I can't thank you more for simply being who you're created to be. You add so much beauty to my life.

Stella Reed, Kristin Lipscomb, Lisa Kai—to my pastor-and-peer sister-friends, each of you has brought such healing and joy to my life and taught me that genuine adult friendships can happen—even in ministry. We are not in competition with one another—we are building the church *together!* You've taught me about cheering each other on and that "better together" is not meant just to be worn on a T-shirt but to be lived out in such a way that it changes the trajectory of each of our lives and causes us to live out the Great Commission and fulfill our purpose—together.

Maria—I'd be in a ditch somewhere, broken and angry, or at least out of ministry completely, if it weren't for you. You are a true mother in the faith to me. You always know when to call, text, or encourage me. You believe in me and see me for who I am. You challenge me when I'm not thinking right and love me in my weakness. You exude Jesus and remind me to continue to walk in His Way, Truth, and Life. You are the salt of the earth, and my life wouldn't be the same without you. I love doing life with you and gleaning from your wisdom and example. Thank you for walking the walk, not just talking the talk. I want to be like you when I'm your age!

Irene—what can I say? As I wrote the chapters in this book, our friendship was growing deeper, and our purpose together was becoming clearer. Thank you for being a friend not just on the mountaintop (and we've stood on a few together) but in what felt like the valley of the shadow of death. You are a friend who won't let me stay in a place of darkness and despair; you turn on the light and show a way out. It's no coincidence that as I wrote these pages, you were helping me avoid the drama in my life, we were forging authentic connection, and we were also beginning to fulfill our purpose together. I can't wait to see what God does with the She Is Free movement as we now lead it together!

Chari—my spiritual midwife, my shield sister (you too, Gaby), and my friend for life. Thank you for believing in me and even seeing *for* me when I wasn't sure what was next. You have the gift of midwifing dreams. You instinctively know what to do next and motivate others to bring the dream into reality, even when the labor is hard and transition makes you want to throw in the towel. Also, you and Esteban let my whole family stay in your house for a week (we are a lot), so we are officially family for life.

Ashley—thank you for the countless audio messages, phone calls, and text messages that bring such life, hope, and joy. You have become such a fount of wisdom, strength, and love in my life. I am so grateful for our friendship. Your encouragement while I was writing this book particularly meant a lot too. It's been a vulnerable ride, and your honest feedback always makes me a better, more thoughtful writer.

Kaylee—who knew (but God) what that drive to the hotel from the airport in Texas would bring? You became our roommate before the pandemic hit and then were stuck with us, literally, for your first year in New York. Now you're stuck by choice, and our whole family loves you so very deeply. You have literally been one of the safest people I know in some of the darkest storms. We have sailed some of them together (hello 2020), and you peacefully stood (knelt down) beside me in a moment that was so difficult and painful for me. When I was embarrassed, you just loved me and removed shame from the room. You brought (and always bring) peace. Kaylee, you are such a gift to my life and this acknowledgment will never do it justice.

Sweet Bailey—I love that everyone thinks you're my daughter. What an honor, truly. You came into our world mid-pandemic and have rallied beside my husband and me in ways no one will ever know. You go above and beyond, and you do it with sheer joy. Your honesty, integrity, and teachability are so beautiful, and you're only just beginning. I love doing life with you and look forward to all the years ahead.

To my Celebrate Recovery Step Study Group—each and every one of you is a gift to my life. I look forward to our Zoom meetings every Wednesday night, and to say that is such a big deal for me. I'm never filled with anxiety to meet, just with holy excitement and expectation for our connection as we support one another, grow, and recover together. Thank you for creating such a safe space to say things out loud I probably never would've said before. I love you all so much.

Nicole, Dawn, and Joy—you all hold very special and trusted places in my heart and life. I cannot express what it means to know you and be known by each of you. Thank you for helping to create genuine connection throughout our years of doing life together, whether we are spending a ton of time together or not. Thank you for having my back—just know that I have yours too. I pray that our various purposes in the kingdom will forever be connected.

Simone, Chris, Mel—my Australian crew—how I miss our times together in the flesh. Each one of you played a significant role in my life and healing in my twenties. You were steady and present and brought so much joy as I walked through one of the darkest nights of my soul. We also just had so much fun together with our countless children and years of growing with one another! Thank you for being friends who weren't just there for the good times but who were there in the hard times too. Love you forever. And Sharalee—those prayer walks and meals together in Bible College changed my life. Our friendship was and is such a treasure to me.

To the Liberty female staff, the She Is Free team, and the girls I get to disciple and walk with—I never would've thought that I could have healthy relationships with women I work and do life with, but each of you has proven me wrong. We're not perfect, but we're giving it our very best. I am so grateful that you're each committed to doing the work in your own hearts and lives, taking ownership and bringing your *whole* self to the table, all while calling out the gold in one another. I am in your corner always.

To new friendships (there's a beautiful handful of you who are just beginning as I write the words on these pages)—thank you for making the effort. I pray our mutual investment begins to bring about great fruit and, of course, a lot of good times in the years to come. I can't wait to see what God does as we choose to create authentic connection and fulfill our purpose together.

To old friendships that are being restored and reconciled— thank you for being brave enough to either reach out or respond when I've extended a hand, to trust God, and to try again. I pray that it will all be to the glory of God.

Jana, Rebekah, and Baker Books—thank you once again for believing in the message that is in and on my life. Through our collective effort, I pray that this book may be found in the right hands, in due season, for such a time as this.

Paul, Zeke, Jesse, and Sam—to the men in my life, thank you for loving me as I am. For giving me space to write, create, embarrass you with my dance moves, and get all teary all the time, whether I'm happy or sad. Each one of you is such a beautiful gift to my life, and I don't think you will ever know the depths of my love for each of you.

And I will never finish a book without thanking the Author of my life, who constantly nudges me along, like a good Father does, to keep going and never give up. As I've written this book, in one of the hardest leadership years of my life, Your Word has truly been a lamp unto my feet and a light unto my path (Ps. 119:105). I'd be lost without Your Word, God, encouraging my soul that there is nothing new under the sun. There is nothing that we're facing here on earth that hasn't been faced. Lord, thank You for loving me in and through each day without fail. Thank You for helping me navigate my friendships and female relationships. Thank You for Your grace, mercy, leading, and encouragement along the way. Thank You for refusing to leave me as I am. Your constant pursuit of my heart changes me. I'd truly be lost without You.

Chapter 1 The Woman Wound

1. Dr. Henry Cloud and Dr. John Townsend, *The Mom Factor* (Grand Rapids: Zondervan, 1996), 18.
2. Cloud and Townsend, *The Mom Factor*, 21.
3. Dictionary.com, s.v. "codependency (*n.*)," accessed March 5, 2021, https://www.dictionary.com/browse/codependency?s=t.

Chapter 2 On the Outside Looking In

1. Beth McCord, *The Enneagram Type 4* (Nashville: Thomas Nelson, 2019), 60.

Chapter 3 Navigating Betrayal

1. Franklin D. Roosevelt, "Franklin D. Roosevelt Quotes," Goodreads, accessed March 5, 2021, https://www.goodreads.com/quotes/1324527-a-smooth-sea-never-made-a-skilled-sailor.
2. Dr. Henry Cloud and Dr. John Townsend, *Boundaries* (Grand Rapids: Zondervan, 2017), 281.
3. "The Five Stages of Grief," Grief.com, accessed March 5, 2021, https://grief.com/the-five-stages-of-grief/.
4. C. S. Lewis, *A Grief Observed* (New York: Seabury Press, 1963), 1.
5. Paul Andrew, "Healthy Boundaries" (sermon), September 29, 2019, Liberty Church, Downtown Manhattan Community, https://libertychurch.com/podcasts/healthy-boundaries-by-paul-andrew/.

Chapter 4 The Truth about Self-Preservation

1. Lexico, s.v. "intimacy (*n.*)," accessed March 10, 2021, https://www.lexico.com/en/definition/intimacy.

Chapter 5 It's Time to Break Up with Drama

1. Lexico, s.v. "insecurity (*n.*)," accessed March 10, 2021, https://www
.lexico.com/en/definition/insecurity.
2. Lexico, s.v. "jealous (*adj.*)," accessed March 10, 2021, https://www.lexico
.com/en/definition/jealous.
3. Lexico, s.v. "competing (*adj.*)," accessed March 10, 2021, https://www
.lexico.com/en/definition/competing.
4. John M. Grohol, PsyD, "What Is Catastrophizing?," PsychCentral, May
17, 2016, https://psychcentral.com/lib/what-is-catastrophizing/.

Chapter 6 No, You Go First

1. Cloud and Townsend, *Boundaries*, 294.

Chapter 7 Creating Authentic Connection—It Doesn't Just Happen

1. Gary Chapman, *The 5 Love Languages* (Chicago: Northfield Publishing,
2010).
2. Ralph Waldo Emerson, "Ralph Waldo Emerson Quotes," Goodreads,
accessed March 10, 2021, https://www.goodreads.com/quotes/27820-the-only
-way-to-have-a-friend-is-to-be.
3. Bessel van der Kolk, MD, *The Body Keeps the Score* (New York: Penguin
Books, 2014), 81.
4. https://churchesthatheal.com/.

Chapter 8 Circles—No, Everyone *Cannot* and *Should Not* Be Your Best Friend

1. C. S. Lewis, *The Four Loves* (New York: Harcourt Brace, 1960), 121.

Chapter 9 Unity in Our Diversity—Together Is Actually Better

1. Lexico, s.v. "friendly fire (*n.*)," accessed March 16, 2021, https://www
.lexico.com/en/definition/friendly_fire.
2. Susan Perlman, "What Is Shalom: The True Meaning," Jews for Jesus,
August 27, 2018, https://jewsforjesus.org/publications/issues/issues-v01-n10
/what-is-shalom-the-true-meaning/.

Chapter 10 Becoming Spiritual Midwives

1. *The American Heritage Dictionary of the English Language*, s.v. "midwife
(*n.*)," accessed March 16, 2021, https://www.ahdictionary.com/word/search
.html?q=midwife.
2. Midwives Alliance North America (MANA), "Home Birth Statement,"
Position Statements, approved September 2012, https://mana.org/pdfs/MANA
PositionStatements.pdf.
3. Lexico, s.v. "advocate (*n., v.*)," accessed March 16, 2021, https://www
.lexico.com/en/definition/advocate.
4. MANA, "Home Birth Statement."

recommended reads

Necessary Endings by Dr. Henry Cloud
Boundaries by Dr. Henry Cloud and Dr. John Townsend
Safe People by Dr. Henry Cloud and Dr. John Townsend
Emotionally Healthy Spirituality by Peter Scazzero
Emotionally Healthy Relationships Day by Day by Peter Scazzero
The Body Keeps the Score by Bessel van der Kolk, MD

about the author

Andi Andrew is the author of *She Is Free, Fake or Follower,* and *Friendship—It's Complicated.* She is also the founding pastor of Liberty Church, a multisite church she pioneered with her husband, Paul, in 2010. In 2015, she launched She Is Free, a movement that exists to engage and equip women to encounter God and expand the kingdom. Currently, Andi's life is focused on raising her four kids in Brooklyn, writing books, creating for her TV show and podcast, *Coffee with Andi,* building Liberty Church, and traveling to invest in churches and lives all around the world.

BREAK FREE FROM THE
LIES HOLDING YOU BACK

Sharing her own intentional journey of finding true freedom by surrendering control of her heart and life to the God who welcomed her with open arms, Andi encourages women to give their pain and brokenness to Jesus. Compassionate and biblically based, *She Is Free* is an invitation to women to step fully into the love that sets them free.

GET TO KNOW
ANDI

ANDIANDREW.COM

Listen on iTunes, Spotify, or wherever you listen to podcasts, or subscribe and watch the TV show on AWKNG+TV, awkngtv.com.

*LIBERTY*church

A GLOBAL FAMILY OF LOCAL CHURCH COMMUNITIES

Visit LibertyChurch.com to find a community near you.

she *is* free

We are a community of women passionate about seeing a movement of wholeness in Christ break out across the earth.

The Vision: She Is Free
Our prayer is for the whole person, spirit, soul, and body.
That *She* would truly be Free. Whole in Christ.

The Mission: She Is Free exists to *engage* and *equip* women to *encounter* God and *expand* the kingdom.

> **Engage:** We desire to help you engage with a real community of women to walk with on the journey of freedom.
>
> **Equip:** We will endeavor to equip you as disciples of Jesus Christ to become more like Him daily.
>
> **Encounter:** We will prayerfully and intentionally create spaces for encounters with God because His presence changes everything.
>
> **Expand:** Our hope is to see you expand the kingdom of God in your sphere of influence here on earth as it is in heaven.

www.sheisfree.com